CONFESSIONS

of a
Direct Resp̌
Copywrite

An "Old School" Advertising Man
Reveals How to
Make Your Marketing
Twice as Effective at Half the Cost –
and Other Secrets of Success
in Business and in Life

By Robert W. Bly

Praise for Bob Bly

"Few e-letters make it past sheer boredom. This one, though, is a sheer classic. Elegant, sage, and funny."

—Lou Wasser

"Thank you for your time and effort to continue your blog posts. I read and enjoy all of them. I also enjoy reading your books that I have. You are appreciated."

—Steve Russell

"If you asked me who the number one 'sell yourself' master in the world is, I'd have to say it is, without question, Bob Bly."

—Michael Masterson

"You are awesome! I will always come to you first for the products that I need. You have class, integrity, brilliance, naturally gifted, and you are second to none! I am impressed with and appreciate your prompt response."

—Adella Pugh

"Once in a blue moon, you get the chance to meet a living legend, one of the great men who has shaped his chosen field. In my unending pursuit of powerful marketing, I came face-to-face with just such a man. Robert Bly is America's Top Copywriter and a genius marketer. He's authored over 70 books for McGraw Hill and others, and gets paid more per word than nearly every author in America. Like all great men, he is a teacher and mentor extraordinaire. He freely shares the secrets of turning marketing into money."

–Dick Larkin

"The best writing teacher in the business!"

–Tom Peric

"Bob, your stuff is always so good that even though I'm retired now, I have to read it!"

–Gary Bencivenga

"You are someone I've grown to admire greatly. You share your knowledge with and encourage people in achieving their dreams, trying new things, and learning tricks of the trade. It's a rare 'guru' in our world today who is thoughtful and kind enough to help up and comers find the path to success. In my opinion, you are the very best. I'm grateful to you."

–Linda Capriotti

"During the past 20 years, Bob Bly has become one of America's leading direct response copywriters. He has probably done more to teach other writers the craft of effective and persuasive writing than anyone else."

–Roger C. Parker

"After considering a number of high-level marketing professionals and reflecting on the matter for several weeks, I made the decision to ask Bob Bly to share the stage with me for my Twin Keys to Wealth-Building Conference. The reason I chose Bob is because I am convinced that he can deliver more tangible value to conference attendees than any other marketing or Internet expert on the planet."

–Robert Ringer, best-selling author

"I love your e-mails. Read every single one of them as they come in."

–Dr. Paul Hartunian

"I have huge admiration for your work. You're one of the few guys out there selling real information – and selling it at a reasonable price! I think what you're doing is head and shoulders above others."

–Mark Joyner

"I receive so many e-mail offers – too many – but Bob always delivers a product worth having. The marketplace for writing and marketing products has become over-hyped; in that environment it's reaffirming to see that Bob continues to stand for a level of quality that matters – and happily, at a price that works. "

–Peg Prideaux

"Watch Bob Bly very closely. He's a very intelligent marketer who knows how to get results and bring in the money!"

–John Kidd

"I have enjoyed all of the books that I have read of yours. I appreciate your no nonsense, take-it-to-the-bank advice that you deliver."
–Nicholas J. Loise, RSVP Chicago

"The Handbook and your bonus are first class. I'm very pleased. You never disappoint."
–Louis J. Wasser, Copywriter

"The product promos you've been sending have plenty of content. I look forward to your e-mails, because they are great idea generators. And your price points are very reasonable. I'd rather pay from $29-$97 for one of your products than the $299 - $500 I've been dishing out to others. Your current business model is brilliant and fair."
–Stanley M. Jackson

"I am delighted every time I take one of your recommendations! You haven't steered me wrong once, and each of your products has been well worth every penny invested."
–Pat Johnson

"I learn a lot from your e-mails even when they point to other products or products you sell. I like learning. Keep it coming."
–Pat McKenzie

"Yours are one of the e-mails that I do enjoy and I order from you as often as I think I can use the help."
–Joe Alagna

"I eagerly anticipate your e-mails – all of them. I've made several purchases. You offer a lot of great advice and insight free. You offer a lot of [other] great advice and insight at very reasonable prices, typically with immediate delivery. Personally, I wouldn't want to miss the opportunity to consider anything you think might be helpful."

–Linda Byam

"You develop a helpful product, describe it in detail, make it easy to access online, post a reasonable price and offer a money back guarantee. Personally, I thank you for your contribution. I've purchased many of your products. And I've made returns. You stand by what you sell, plus."

–Lynn Roberts

"What we receive free from you and others has the potential to ignite countless ideas - priceless ones on occasion. The opportunity to in turn purchase something from the 'sales' e-mails is complimentary to you sharing so much priceless info with us – your willing subscribers. Press on and keep allowing us to benefit from your years of experience however you share it."

–Eddie Stephen

*"In work, do what you enjoy.
In family life, be completely present."*

—Lao Tzu

"That which one man knows can be taught to others."

—George Clason, The Richest Man in Babylon

*"Men are anxious to improve their circumstances,
but are unwilling to improve themselves;
therefore they remain bound."*

—James Allen, As a Man Thinketh

This book is for
Bill and Jodi Sterling

TABLE OF CONTENTS

Acknowledgments

Thanks to those subscribers to my e-newsletter The Direct Response Letter who asked me questions and suggested topics that sparked many of the essays in these chapters.

Introduction

For well over a decade, I've published a twice-weekly e-newsletter that goes to about 65,000 subscribers.

Originally I dispensed strictly marketing advice. But then I broadened the scope to encompass more areas of business success and life in general.

Then a problem arose: as I get older, I get crankier and more irritable. I hold to the belief that older people as a rule are correct more often than younger people, because, as my favorite comic Louis CK has observed, their opinions are based on more information.

This increasingly grouchy and cynical attitude began to assert itself in my online essays, which I feared would alienate my subscribers. More and more of my essays became what is known in information marketing as "rants" – complains against the stupidity of the status quo.

But to my great surprise, my subscribers loved these rants and opinionated ramblings – and the more personal they were, the better they loved them.

Once I realized that, I continued to indulge myself. And today, my e-newsletter is probably a 70/30 mixture of personal opinions on important business and life topics vs. straightforward tips on marketing topics.

Is this the best advice in the world on business and life? Probably not, but it is the best I can give you, based on my experience as a marketer, entrepreneur, and writer since 1979. You can read my bio at the back of the book, along with testimonials from my e-newsletter subscribers, to determine whether I am worth listening to.

I continue to write and distribute the essays online, so if you have a question, e-mail it to me and I may, if I feel qualified and able, answer it in a future issue: rwbly@bly.com

Some of the essays my readers tell me they liked best are collected in three books I published as Kindle e-books and CreateSpace paperbacks. This one is the fourth in the series. The first three are *Don't Wear a Cowboy Hat Unless You are a Cowboy; The Blunt and Brutal Truth About Business and Life;* and *Bob Bly's Little Blue Book of Business Wisdom.* Like this one, these are also available on www.amazon.com

Note: Almost all the essays in this new book were first published in my e-newsletter; a few were written for e-newsletters published by my affiliate partners, and a couple in my columns for the trade publications.

I typically place most of my books with mainstream publishing houses and usually eschew self-publishing. But I self-publish these essay collections mainly because (a) I don't think a major publishing house would go for them yet (b) my subscribers and other readers seem to want them. I'm guessing that since you are reading this one, maybe you do too – and I hope you enjoy it.

In addition, you can get all my future e-mail essays free by signing up for my e-newsletter, The Direct Response Letter. When you sign up, you also get 4 free bonus reports totaling 200 pages with a retail value of over $100. Details are on the sign-up page, which you can reach by typing www.bly.com/reports into your browser, and also at the back of this book.

It's my hope that by reading this book, you will in plain and easy-to-read language get advice and ideas that can help you:

- Make and save more money.
- Have greater freedom and control of your life.
- Enjoy meaningful work that you absolutely love.
- Improve your business and personal relationships.
- Become financially secure.
- Do what you want and avoid doing things you don't want to do.

I sincerely believe that even if you only get one good idea for improving just one of the areas named above, it will pay back the modest cost of this book tenfold or more – not a bad return on your reading investment.

CHAPTER 1

Avoid This Mistake When Migrating to New Media

It's ironic.

Direct response guys by far know more about what works in marketing than anyone else, because we generate tangible results on every promotion. And these results are measured.

Yet more and more marketers are bypassing direct response today in favor of what is hot and trendy — specifically branding, content marketing, digital marketing, and social media.

For instance, my friend BC, a veteran direct marketing pro, recently wrote me an e-mail. He says:

"I've had so many clients insist on dropping what they call 'traditional' media for digital and social media, only to have a harsh awakening as their response plummets.

"One such client is a small community college who was struggling during the recession. They were down to just under 7,000 students and state funding was cut.

"Teaching jobs were on the line. We launched a campaign with traditional media with the right message. And in just 2 enrollment periods — spring and fall of the same year — we raised enrollment to just over 11,000 students ... an increase of 57%.

"We sustained that number and even moved it up a notch or two for 3 years. Then the college's Marketing Committee got comfortable and bored, fired us, and hired a digital/social media agency.

"The new media agency produced disastrous results. Enrollment went from just over 11,000 students down to 6,500 students in 2 enrollment cycles. The last numbers I learned of were below 4,500 students.

"Now the college doesn't have an ad budget, and most of the Marketing Committee, who were also professors and instructors, have been let go due to lack of funds.

"The college's Marketing Director was moved from his office suite in the main building to an office on a remote side of the campus.

"This is why I always tell clients to ease into 'new media' slowly – and test, test, and test!"

I urge you to consider BC's story and advice carefully. He is a top pro and he knows what he is talking about.

In my view, this myopic college Marketing Director, who had BC's vast expertise at his disposal, starved to death with a loaf of bread under each arm.

Apparently, these professors are not the only marketers failing to be cautious when transitioning from old-school print media to digital.

Subscriber DG writes:

"Don't throw the baby out with the bathwater!

"For the past 25 years, we used old fashioned snail-mail brochures to promote our engineering seminars.

"The recipient is invited to sign up online. In the early days, we even used a live registration firm. Online is even simpler.

"We tried purchased e-mail lists a couple of times, but the response was abysmal. However, our own compiled lists – past clients and others – do quite well.

"The results: over 12,000 students and probably over a million mailing pieces. The extra revenues nicely enhanced the retirement accounts.

"Now I am doing classes through a small training company. They mail an old fashioned catalog several times a year, with on-line registration for the response. Quite successful."

"So direct response is NOT dead, at least in my world."

Subscriber DK tells a similar cautionary tale:

"3 years ago I had a client who specialized in laser surgery to clear toenail fungus. Not glamorous, but necessary.

"I got them a 2-month Outdoor paper Poster campaign ... 10' X 20' signs ... you might consider them billboards. Valued at over $100,000, we got a two month deal for $30,000.

"Ads ran in Feb and March. In November that same year people were flocking to the clinics saying they remembered the Outdoor posters.

"The next spring, since our campaign worked so well, the client dumped us and pumped $25,000 into online somewhere.

"And what did they get for their 25 grand? About 6 likes, no sales, no phone calls, and no one visiting any of their six health clinics. Nada.

"Haven't seen a ripple of activity from them since.

"Digital/On-line/Social are nice add-ons in moderation when they have been vetted and tested, but they are not a panacea for all that ails struggling businesses."

Takeaways:

1–Traditional print still works some of the time. Digital can work some of the time. Sometimes they work well together.

2–Don't throw out a campaign that is still working just because you are bored with it, because if it is still working, your prospects obviously AREN'T bored with it.

3–Test new channels, media, and tactics gradually and cautiously. Stick your toe into the water first, before driving into the deep end of the pool.

CHAPTER 2

Seven Rules of Effective Retail Advertising

Several of my readers have asked me for advertising tips for retailing.

And since I don't write retail copy, I turned to my pal Brian Croner, who was kind enough to provide these "7 Rules of Effective Retail Advertising."

1–Hard sell out-pulls soft sell. An independently owned store doesn't have the ad budget of a big chain. So one ad needs to do the job of 10 or 20. Your ad has to get more attention than your larger competitors and has to create a sense of urgency and a fear of loss.

2–Use bargain appeals. Whether your prices are better than your competition isn't relevant. Make your customers BELIEVE you have great deals. This could be something as simple as "60% OFF RETAIL!" ("Retail" can be any number.)

Or have some loss leaders available so you can make the claim legally by saying; "Some items SOLD AT OR BELOW COST!" These bargain appeals work!

3–Always have an event or sale. "I have skeptics ask me all the time. 'Won't you lose credibility if you run a sale all the time?'" says Brian. "The answer is: no, you won't."

For instance, when someone is in need of a new mattress or piece of furniture, they LOOK for SALES and EVENTS! Your advertising has to appeal to the next group of prospects ready to buy your products NOW.

4–Have a start date for your event; e.g., "STARTS FRIDAY at 10am!" Brian says he uses this hook in over 30 markets and it works in all of them. It generates excitement and makes people plan to go to the store.

5–Create a limited time frame for your event. "Almost all the furniture stores we have worked with were going to close on Black Friday," says Brian.

"Our clients run 10 or 12-hour sales on Black Friday. The event is hyped all week long through Thanksgiving Day on local media. A recent store who just signed on with us did around $45,000 on Black Friday in a town of only 13,000 occupants!"

6–Buy media wisely. You're in the business of purchasing customers – not space, not time, not "likes."

And don't believe for a minute that local radio, local television, and your local newspaper are "obsolete". These mediums still have good circulation and loyal audiences.

If you want to add social media, go into it slowly and measure the results carefully. Both Brian and I have watched multiple businesses nosedive when they pulled away from what was working with "traditional media" and invested most or all of their ad budgets into new media.

7–Repeat your successes. When elements of an advertisement work, you keep it, repeat it, and try to improve upon it. If your "48-Hour Stock Reduction Sale" worked this year, it will most likely work again next year.

Brian Croner is the owner/CEO of Marketing Resource Group, a full service advertising agency with heavy expertise in retail. They can be found on the Web at www.mresourcegroup.com.

CHAPTER 3

Easy Reading is Hard Writing

RS, an ad agency creative direct, wrote the following in a recent article on branding:

"Today, the emerging big brands among us are those that are bringing the future to fruition – changing how we exist, interact, and sustain our lives. They're making social networks, self-driving cars, hover boards, and holograms.

"And most interesting of all, this new class of brand is led by a visionary founder with a particular philosophy, not by a corporate entity acting out a product roadmap against established brand guidelines and architecture.

"People like Elon Musk, Evan Spiegel, and Mark Zuckerberg are pursuing innovation across product and business lines that sometimes don't organize quite as neatly under a parent company as the businesses of yesteryear had, and instead are branded in siloes."

Is this good writing?

I would bet that when RS read his draft, he was glowing with pride at his highfalutin, breathless prose.

But in my forthcoming book on writing, I will use it as an example of how NOT to write ... and in my writing seminars my students call this one, "What did he say?"

To me, it stinks, because RS violates an important rule of good writing:

"Write to express – not to impress."

F. Scott Fitzgerald mocked Hemingway for Ernie's simple, basic vocabulary and plain, unadorned style.

"He thinks I don't know the ten dollar words," Hemingway said of Fitzgerald's criticism. "I do. I just prefer the $1 words instead."

When I first started teaching business and technical writing seminars for corporate clients, I would occasionally have an attendee who, when I said simple and plain writing is best, argued with me.

They said they had been taught all their life to write in a formal, corporate style – and the conversational style I was teaching in the class was wrong and inappropriate for business.

I would show these naysayers the Flesch readability test; they usually remained unpersuaded.

But when I got into direct response copywriting, I had finally had objective proof – not just subjective opinion – to support my assertion that simple writing is the best writing … at least when it comes to communication.

And the proof is this: almost without exception, virtually every successful direct response promotion is written in clear, concise, conversational copy.

It's the style used by John Forde … Clayton Makepeace … Richard Armstrong … Ivan Levison … Paul Hollingshead … Steve Slaunwhite … and just about every top six- and seven-figure copywriter I know.

Why? Because it is plain English that virtually always gets the best response – proving that when it comes to communicating, simple writing is the best writing.

And it's not just my personal opinion that clear writing trumps ornate writing, and that plain language communicates more effectively than big words.

It's a tested fact.

So there!

And if you prefer my plain and unadorned prose style to RS's pompous, overblown one ... and you strive to attain a clear, conversational writing style that makes you a pleasure to read and easy to understand instead of a pompous blowhard like RS ... check out my book *The Elements of Business Writing* (Pearson).

Okay, maybe "pompous blowhard" is a little harsh on RS. Then again – maybe not. Because I know guys like him in advertising. And they love to use a $10 word when a $1 word would get their message across faster and better. It makes them think the ideas are expressing are both more profound and more novel than they actually are.

CHAPTER 4

Must Copywriters Do More Than Just Write Copy?

Subscriber JA writes, "I am finding clients who say they want a copywriter, and then ask for additional services such as design and Web development, including programming. How do you sell them on just the writing aspect that they need first and foremost?"

I do three simple things that solve the problem easily and neatly.

First, I send them a link to my FAQ page where it states the following:

"Q: What if I need graphics, not just the copy? Do you work with an artist?"

"A: I work with the best direct-mail artists and Web designers in the world, but it's not a package deal. After you hire me, I'll give you some recommendations on the right artist for your job and you can come to terms with him or her on your own. I can also work with your artist or Web developer, if you prefer. Either way is fine with me."

I stole this language from Richard Armstrong. We are in essence saying, "We can get you the other parts of the project you need, but we don't act as an ad agency or manage the project for you."

Second, I make it easy for the client to find vendors who can provide whatever they need that I don't do – by posting a vendor directory page on my site:

http://www.bly.com/newsite/Pages/vendors.php

When a client asks "What will a mailing list or design for my Website cost?" I don't go out and get a quote from the vendor. I point the client to the vendor's page link above – and tell them they have to contact the vendor directly to get the pricing.

Third, after all this, there will still be a few clients who will only hire you to write their copy if you also act as a digital agency and deliver the entire package.

In such situations, you can say one of two things: Yes. Or no.

If you are in such demand as a copywriter that you have many more potential clients than you can handle, then sticking by your guns, saying you write copy only, and refusing to provide full agency services is easy.

That's the option I have chosen: fill my lead pipeline to overflowing so I only have to take the jobs I want. And projects where the client wants me to "do the whole thing" are jobs I do not want. So I turn them down.

On the other hand, if you are hungry and need the work, turning away good assignments from clients who demand a turnkey service is more difficult, and you may choose to give them what they want. It's up to you.

CHAPTER 5

Is Facebook "Online Advertising" or "Social Networking"?

According Duke University's School of Business's recent CMO survey, 44.1% of marketers said they are unable to show the impact of social media.

Another 35.6% say there is a quantitative impact but cannot measure hard numbers for sales ROI and other key metrics.

Bottom line: about 8 out 10 marketers surveyed haven't realized the ROI they expected from social media, dampening their desire to invest more time and money in the channel.

Whenever I share this, I always get responses from people who tell me they can measure social ROI and are crushing it on social.

But 99 times out of 100, it turns out that they are talking about boosted posts and paid advertising on Facebook ... and most recently, Twitter.

One can argue – and I am that one – that FB and Twitter ads are not really "social media" or "social marketing."

They are online advertising, same as pay-per-click ads on Google or Bing, banner ads on Websites, and ads in e-zines.

When I question whether social media works or produces a decent ROTI (return on time invested), I am not questioning the efficacy of FB paid ads – because I already know they can work like gangbusters.

What I'm questioning is whether endless blabbing and chatter on Facebook, Snapchat, and other social networks generates a good ROI.

Well, the Duke surveys says 8 out of 10 CMOs cannot confirm a positive ROI from their social media.

Now, whenever I say this, someone will blast me, pointing out that Grant Cardone is "crushing it" on Snapchat and Gary Vaynerchuk is doing likewise on multiple social networks – as if this invalidates the Duke survey findings.

Well, it doesn't. Because there are exceptions to everything, and in social media ROI, Grant and Gary are two of a small group of exceptions who are in fact making money with social.

But for the majority of marketers, social media remains an unproven medium that often sucks time and funds that would be better spend on other activities – such as e-mail marketing and direct mail.

Yes, it doesn't cost a lot of money, but I contend social marketing has a poor ROTI – return on time invested. And since time is so precious, blabbing on Snapchat or tweeting half a dozen times a day without generating hard dollar revenues online is to me a waste.

By the way, if you think I am behind the times or even daft because I recommend direct mail over social media, the Direct Marketing Association reports that every dollar spent on direct mail produces on average $12 in revenues based on lifetime customer value, which is the second the highest ROI of all B2C marketing channels after e-mail.

CHAPTER 6

Can You Post Client Work on Your Site?

Subscriber GR writes:

"When I send clients an agreement, it states using samples is important to my business.

"I have a client who doesn't want the work I do for him displayed on my site; I'm thinking he's worried about his competitors.

"I have never done an e-book for a client...so this certain sample would be important to me, as future clients may ask if I've done one.

"Since you are an expert, what are your thoughts to solve this problem?"

My feeling is you should NEVER put in your agreements that you automatically have the right to use the promotion you wrote for the client to market your own services.

Why not?

Because some clients want their marketing – or the fact that you wrote it for them – to be confidential.

They want to keep what they are doing under wraps – and not put it on display where it is easily imitated or knocked off.

That is their right ... and for them may be the sensible path.

So if your copywriting contract requires clients to let you use their samples to promote your services, many prospects may not hire you because of that contract clause.

So I never, ever include it in the agreement.

What happens is that once the promotion is produced, I tell them it looks so great, may I please post it as a sample on my Website's portfolio?

At that point 95% give permission to post what you did for them on your online portfolio. And so – problem solved. They will even give you a PDF of the finished artwork which makes it a snap to post the promotion on your site.

As for the 5% who say they do not want you to show the work to others, you absolutely should comply with their wishes – and do not share the sample with anyone under any circumstance – as much as you want to.

This is the right way to handle sharing and display of client samples. You do not want to get a reputation for violating client confidentiality, which you will if you show client work to others without permission.

Years ago a consultant friend of mine produced a small brochure where he listed the names of some of his clients on one of the panels – without asking these clients if it was OK to do so.

He received an angry and threatening complaint from one major client's legal department saying he did not have permission to use their name – and telling him to immediately remove it from the brochures.

Because he did a large print run, he spent several evenings going through the brochures one by one and erasing the company's name using liquid white-out – which looked pretty awful.

In another example, I worked for a Fortune 500 defense contractor. We printed an outrageously expensive and elaborate color brochure on an electronic subassembly used in Air Force F-16 fighter jets.

To make the picture more interesting, we photographed the assembly with its cover off to show the components.

Well, we got a stern letter from the Department of Defense saying the power ratings on the components were legible, and therefore we were revealing classified information.

The solution: At great expense, we made sticky labels of the same equipment photographed with the cover on, and then pasted them one at a time, by hand, over the original photos in 2,000 copies of the brochure.

Lesson: always get permission first.

CHAPTER 7

Are Rich Customers More Difficult to Satisfy?

Are rich people who spend a lot of money with you often prima donnas who are demanding and impossible to please?

From what I've seen, this is sometimes true in the world of consumer marketing, whether at a luxury resort, 5-star gourmet restaurant, or exclusive London men's shop selling bespoke suits.

But in business, I have found quite the opposite to be true – the more money a client spends with you, the more respectful, polite, and easy to work with they will be ... because the more they value you.

In business the converse is also true: the client who talks you down in price and gets you cheap turns out to be the most difficult, demanding, hard to deal with, and impossible to please.

My theory as to why this should be so in business is as follows ...

If the client with deep pockets is an entrepreneur, part of his success is that he takes pains to treat people fairly and with respect, so they in turn will like him and give him their best work.

And if your client is with a big corporation with deep pockets, then he is usually a full-time professional marketer, and he knows how to deal with vendors in our field – and has the budget to afford them without undue hardship.

On the other hand, some entrepreneurs with shallow pockets often haggle over your price, not because they are jerks, but because they are on shoestring budgets.

They also question what you do at every step. Not because they want to be pick or difficulty.

But because they do desperately need their marketing campaign to work, and inexperienced clients may find it difficult to let go of their own judgement in favor of an expert's, like yours.

Therefore, the well-heeled clients with big budgets who pay generous fees are so often the easiest and most cooperative to work with ... while the tiny accounts who have to watch every penny can sometimes be difficult, demanding, and contentious.

Are there exceptions to all this? Of course. I write copy for a number of small businesses whose owners I am incredibly fond of.

But overall, the generalizations I just made turn out to be true more often than they are wrong.

Do you find they hold true in your business as well as mine?

CHAPTER 8

The Essentialist Way

In his best-selling book "Essentialism: The Disciplines Pursuit of Less" (Crown Business), Greg McKeown preaches his philosophy of Essentialism as the path to having a better and more rewarding life.

The core idea of Essentialism is, in McKeown's words, this:

> "There are far more activities and opportunities in the world than we have the time and resources to invest in.
>
> "And although many of them may be good, or even very good, the fact is that most are trivial and few are vital.
>
> **"Only when you give yourself permission to stop trying to do it all, to stop saying yes to everyone, can you make your highest contribution towards the things that really matter."**

If you know people who pursue a primary goal, activity, or mission with laser-like focus – whether it's building a business or accumulating wealth – they are almost surely, with rare exceptions, Essentialists.

If you know people who volunteer for everything, have a calendar filled with diverse activities, pursue a dozen hobbies and interests, and sign up for every committee on every worthwhile organization under the sun – I can virtually assure you that they are not Essentialists.

I only came across McKeown's book a couple of months ago. But I have been an Essentialist my entire adult life.

I focus, to the exclusion of almost everything else, on just the few things that matter most to me – my business and my clients, writing, and my family.

Yes, I would like to do more. But as McKeown correctly points out, our time, attention, energy, and bandwidth are finite.

So if you try to do everything, you accomplish – and get good at – almost nothing.

"The overwhelming reality is: we live in a world where almost everything is worthless and a very few things are exceptionally valuable," McKeown writes.

"We can choose how to spend our energy and time. We can't have or do it all."

He quotes John Maxwell, who has written, "You cannot overestimate the unimportance of practically everything."

Marcus Aurelius said it this way: "If thou wouldst know contentment, let thy deeds be few."

Old Russian proverb: "He who hunts both foxes, and rabbits, catches neither foxes, nor rabbits."

The way I put it is this: If you are someone who is "all over the place," you will never really get to the one place you want to go.

By the way, my dedication to Essentialism does not mean I make zero contribution to worthy causes outside my small number of core activities.

But I do so in the most time-efficient manner — by donating money rather than my time to these worthy causes.

By focusing just on my business, I make more money. In turn, this enables me to make bigger contributions to curing cancer, feeding the hungry, and other things that are important but that I do not have the bandwidth to participate in directly.

CHAPTER 9

Why the Wide Disparity in Copywriting Fees?

The range of fees freelance copywriters charge today is all over the lot – and may seem puzzling to you as a potential buyer of copywriting services.

On the high-end, top industry pros can command huge fees to write magalogs, direct mail packages, landing pages, video sales letters, and other long-copy assignments.

On the low end, you can find beginners who charge $300 or less to write a landing page, and as little as $50 for online articles. If you outsource overseas, you can even find writers to do online articles for $5 each (you can imagine how good they are).

So which option – the expensive pro or the bargain-basement beginner – should you choose? It really depends on you, your business, your goals, and your budget.

If your budget is tight – and you don't have the time or inclination to write your own copy – and you view copy as merely words on a page or screen – then by all means hire the cheapest copywriter you can find.

After all, anyone can put words on a screen or page. Anyone can write. We all do.

On the other hand, perhaps you want your copy to generate specific marketing results – including more click-throughs, increased Web traffic, higher conversion rates, or more leads or sales.

That's something relatively few copywriters know how to do well. If you've ever hired an inexpensive beginning copywriter, you know that what I am saying is true.

When you depend on copy to make money for you, then you might consider hiring a copywriter with more experience, greater knowledge, and a long track record of writing profitable promotions for clients big and small.

Why? Because with any kind of online or offline marketing that generates direct sales or leads, strongly crafted copy is an investment, not an expense.

For instance, say you have a landing page generating $100,000 a year in revenues with a 2% conversion rate.

If stronger copy increases that conversion rate from just 2% to 3%, that copy will generate increased sales of $50,000 within 12 months – and half a million dollars more over the next decade!

So what are you looking for in a copywriter – "words on a page or screen" – or strong, hard-selling copy that drives response rates through the roof?

I close with these words of wisdom from the late English philosopher John Ruskin:

"There is hardly anything in the world that some man cannot make a little worse and sell a little cheaper, and the people who consider price only are this man's lawful prey."

CHAPTER 10

A Common Mistake in Copywriting

Niraj, CEO of something called Hiver, recently sent me an e-mail on "7 words to avoid in e-mail."

And #1 on his list was "you."

This is absolutely the worst writing advice ever given – because YOU is arguably one of two the most powerful words in the English language – the other being FREE.

The e-mail from Hiver is part of an insidious practice that has been going on for years: People who have absolutely no idea of what they are talking about giving marketing advice.

Why doesn't Niraj like the word "you." He says people might find it "accusatory," which is pure nonsense.

If he was a direct marketer, he would know, from testing, that "you" works. It engages the reader like nothing else can. After all, the thing people care most about is themselves.

Similarly, I have people tell me they do not use "free" in e-mail because it is (a) too low-brow and (b) triggers spam filters.

Again, we have tested "free" in e-mail extensively and find that, just as it does in print, the word free increases response.

It is not too lowbrow. Almost everyone wants free stuff. Using the more formal "complimentary" as a substitute for "free" weakens your copy and depresses response.

CHAPTER 11

How to Prevent Typos in Your Marketing Materials

Aside from some direct marketers who believe a deliberate typo on page 1 of a promotion can actually increase response, 99% of marketers do not want to see embarrassing typos or spelling errors in their marketing materials. But how do you prevent it?

The copywriter cannot do it alone, although I carefully proof and spell-check my copy – several times.

The reason your copywriter can't take sole responsibility for proofreading is that by the time he proofs the final draft, he has written, rewritten, and edited the text so many times, reading it has become somewhat routine and automatic to him, and that can make him miss errors.

You, the marketer, have the same problem: By the time the promo is ready to print or post, you've read it so many times, you too will likely be unable to inspect it as carefully as proofreading demand.

That is why I urge you to give the final Web-ready or camera-ready artwork to at least one other person in your organization – preferably someone who knows grammar and spelling – to proofread it as well.

Because she has never seen it before, she will be much more likely to catch errors than you and I.

And although it is up to you whether you do so, I strongly suggest you e-mail to your copywriter a PDF of the promotion in layout form.

This allows me to check that all components are in the right place, and that the design is as effective as it can be.

I also give the layout to my proofreader for a final proofing on our end. I then give any additional corrections and comments to the client, and finally the promotion is posted or mailed.

However, the client is responsible for the final proofreading. I am not liable for errors and typos, because a writer, having written and rewritten the piece many time already, is the least effective person for final proofing. An outside pair of eyes is infinitely better.

Anyway, there is no charge for this careful review and checking of the test and design – it is a free service for my clients.

I truly appreciate and urge my clients to keep me current on the results. I will often suggest test ideas or improvements to the client at no cost, so as to maximize response.

CHAPTER 12

Why Your Direct Mail Package Should Include a Response Device

At last once a week, a client asks me if it's okay for them to leave the business reply card (BRC) out of their next direct mail package.

I almost always tell them that to omit the reply element from a DM package is a huge mistake – one this can significantly repress response and send their ROI from the mailer from the stratosphere into the basement.

They have two arguments to support their desire to deep-six the reply card.

First, they are on a budget. So if they can eliminate the reply card, they'll save on printing and postage.

The problem is that they end up saving a few hundred dollars at best ... and in the process often lose out on a thousands of dollars in leads, orders, and new customers – penny-wise and pound-foolish, in my view.

The second argument goes something like this: "In today's digital age, paper reply elements are old hat; people want to respond online, not mail a card."

The modern customer, they inform me, prefers to go to a landing page URL and download the free report, e-book, or other lead magnet being offered.

While it's true that prospects today want to be given the option of responding online by visiting a landing page, here's what not one marketer in a hundred knows that my colleagues and I do:

Namely, that even if very few recipients actually use the paper reply element, just having the physical reply card in the letter actually boosts the number of total responses we get both online and via phone call to our 800 number!

Reason: When the prospect opens a direct mail envelope and sees a physical reply card or form, it is a visual signal that says to the recipient, "Hey, this is not just content or branding. This is one of those letters that you are supposed to respond to!"

As a result, overall response rate is lifted, which is what you want, and you will find that all three reply mechanisms – reply card, landing page URL, and phone – get a boost in usage.

Without an enclosed reply form or card, not only do you miss out on postal responses from prospects who prefer the mail for replying. But your inbound phone responses and landing page conversion will be lower, too. And who wants that?

In a similar vein, remember that print ads back in the day had response coupons, which on average boosted leads and orders around 15%.

With the advent of toll-free 800 numbers and URLs, advertisers began dropping coupons from their print ads.

But guess what?

Those who left coupons in the ads found that this actually still increases total ad response – including from both 800 numbers and the Web!

Again, the coupon is a graphic indicator that says to the reader: "This is not just an image, branding, or content ad. This is one of those ads where when you respond you get something in return."

Takeaway: In the digital age, direct mail should ideally offer all 3 reply mechanisms: phone, landing page URL, and yes, a paper reply element – typically either a BRC or order form with business reply envelope (BRE).

CHAPTER 13

Every Business Has Its Problems – No Exceptions!

Is freelance copywriting being oversold as a business opportunity, with those who write about it looking through rose-colored glasses?

Well, in some ways yes. But so is just about every business opportunity and profession under the sun.

One of the problems with writings about freelance copywriting in particular is you always heard the great success stories ... but no one is forthcoming about the bad stuff that happens to copywriters, too.

Nothing in this life is all sunshine and flowers. *Every job, career, business opportunity, or small business has its pros and cons.*

Freelance copywriting is no exception. There are a lot of good things. But also some bad things.

The good far outnumber the bad; if that were not the case, I wouldn't still be a freelance copywriter after nearly 4 decades in the business.

But everyone tells you only about the good stuff. And only a few willingly tell the total truth – the bad along with the good.

One famous copywriter recently wrote to me and said:

"I'll tell you a story about the week between Christmas and New Year's that shows what life is like for a freelance copywriter like myself!

"This happened about 15 years ago. I just finished a magalog for one of the big financial publishers a few days before Christmas.

"They got back to me on the day before Christmas and said it needed a massive rewrite. So I spent that whole week between Christmas and New Year's working 12-hour days trying to rewrite the whole thing from scratch.

"Then on December 31st, they called me—before I'd even submitted the revised copy—and said, 'Look, we've decided this is so far off base, we'd rather pay you the fee and kill it.'

"The worst part was knowing I could've spent that week relaxing!"

The fact is, almost anything you can do for a living in this world has both pros and cons.

Freelance copywriting is no exception.

And that's the way it is.

For the full story on the real truth about freelance copywriting – the good, the bad, and the ugly – click here now: http://www.copywritingclientsfromhell.com/

I love copywriting, for the most part. But if you go into it – or anything else, for that matter – do so with your eyes wide open.

CHAPTER 14

John Steinbeck's "Lost" Writing Secret

One of the factors that can elevate your writing to the next level of effectiveness and power is enthusiasm.

By that I mean enthusiasm both for the subject matter as well as the particular piece you are writing, whether it's an essay, article, book, ad, blog post, or sales letter.

When you are enthusiastic about what you are writing, that excitement and caring will shine through in your words.

But some writers tell me that mustering enthusiasm is a problem, because they don't think what they are writing is unique, valuable, or important.

A sales trainer writing a book on selling so he could get more speaking gigs said to me, "There are already so many books on selling, I question why I am even bothering to produce one more."

And I see his point.

A copywriter working on a promotion for a prostate supplement told me, "There are so many products in this category, and they all seem to have the same ingredients – plus, not having prostate problems myself, I can't say from personal experience that this one actually works."

Well, the great novelist John Steinbeck had a simple solution to putting enthusiasm into your writing even in situations such as these.

He said: ""The writer must believe that what he is doing is the most important thing in the world. And he must hold to this illusion even when he knows it is not true."

For instance, I am not a truck mechanic, so I am never going to use the tools for fleet maintenance my client sells. I wouldn't even know how.

But DS, my client, loves what he sells. Tools and truck maintenance are his passion. He communicates that love to me when I interview him, and so I am able to muster what I call "temporary enthusiasm."

You see, you do not have to love everything you are writing about. What you DO have to do is become excited and jazzed about it during the weeks or months you are writing about it – "temporary enthusiasm."

And that you can do. I do it all the time. You can too.

Now, there are two additional methods in addition to "temporary enthusiasm" that can help you have a more positive attitude toward your writing assignments.

The first is to gravitate toward clients whose products or industries you absolutely love, or if not love, at least really like or are interested in.

For instance, one of my copywriting clients is a major science fiction publisher. I love SF, so doing their work is pure joy for me.

Another makes chemical agents for fire suppression. While I don't "love" fire suppression, I am a chemical engineer, and I DO love writing about interesting technology – and theirs is indeed fascinating.

The second technique for avoiding lack of enthusiasm in your writing is to turn down projects in which you have zero interest if not outright disdain.

In 1982, the first year of my freelance copywriting career, when things were lean, a mainstream book publisher asked me to write 5 direct mail package, one each for a different book.

Thrilled to get the call, I asked him the subject matter.

When he replied that it was hunting, I was crestfallen, and – painfully, because I needed the work, the portfolio samples, and the money – I turned it down.

Why? Because I love animals, and knew I could not write with enthusiasm or credibility about the joy of killing them – something I would never do.

The client was actually offended, because he thought I was saying hunting is wrong or evil.

(Quickest way to start an argument in this world: tell a hunter you think hunting is wrong.)

I was not saying that hunting was immoral. If people want to hunt, they have the legal right to do so. I just don't understand why they would do it ... or how they could get pleasure out of it.

I simply don't like the idea of hunting, and while I am not doing anything to stop it, I certainly am not going to promote it, either.

P.S. On a recent Christmas Eve, a small animal – I think it was a squirrel but am not 100% sure; it MIGHT have been a cat – darted out into the road in front of my car.

I had a choice: run over the animal and continue safely, or make an emergency swerve to avoid hitting it.

I swerved, hit a telephone poll, and totaled my beloved 2008 Toyota Prius (fortunately, I have a spare Prius).

Some people who hear this story think I am an idiot and should just have run over the animal.

I tell them I had no time to think about it and had to make a quick decision.

But if I had more time to make the decision or the ability to think 1,000X faster, I still would have done the same thing: swerve and wreck my car rather than hurt an animal.

If that makes me stupid in your eyes, I hope it does not lower your opinion of me TOO much.

CHAPTER 15

Unlock the Gold Mine Hidden in Your Content

There is hidden gold in content you have already written.

For most writers, that content sits idle in file cabinets and on hard drives – wasting away and not earning them a dime.

Except, in the explosive information marketing industry, content owners can now generate thousands of dollars of additional profits from content they already have!

For instance, over the years, I developed many documents used in my freelance writing business – model letters, client agreements, checklists, press releases, invoices, and so on.

One day, I said to myself, "Why not sell all these documents, which I already have and are proven to work, to other copywriters and aspiring copywriters as an e-book?"

It took me only 2 hours to assemble these documents, all sitting on my hard drive as Word files, into an e-book manuscript.

I gave the manuscript to a graphic artist to design a cover and the interior pages, and turn it into an e-book with the title "The Copywriter's Toolkit," which he did for $200.

Result? To date, we have sold 2,317 copies generating $117,663 in gross revenues – all from content I had already written.

And you wonder why so many people just love online info marketing!

3 tips I give to writers and others who create intellectual content that can help you sell your words and ideas over and over again, quickly and affordably, online:

1–Keep everything you write, published and unpublished, with clearly labeled files in easy-to-remember directories and subdirectories. You have to know where your content is stored and be able to retrieve it in electronic format quickly.

2–Same goes for speeches, seminars, workshops, lectures, Webinars, podcasts, and the like; make sure it is recorded and you get a master of the mp3 or mp4 file.

3–Retain all rights to your written and spoken content. Negotiate this with the producers and publishers if not offered automatically.

One way to do this with written content: Type the words "first rights only" in the upper left corner of every article you submit to a magazine, newsletter, or Website. By doing so, you retain the right to use it as you wish once it appears that publication.

Content creators who either give up the rights to their material or do not save and store it properly for easy retrieval are throwing away the potential fortune hidden in their "content goldmines." Remember, I made over $117K selling a bunch of documents, forms, and letters I had already written – creating nothing original for my Toolkit!

CHAPTER 16

Terrorists Almost Killed my Mother

On January 7, 2017, a gunman opened fire in the Fort Lauderdale, Florida airport killing 5 people in the baggage area.

What makes this personal for me is that my mother and her boyfriend were standing in that same baggage claim in the same airport one week earlier.

Many people, and I am one of them, complain too much over minor things.

For instance, I lose my cool when the traffic going into NYC is at a standstill or I lose Internet service for 20 minutes.

Yet if my mother had left for Florida a week later, she might be dead today.

Global terrorism has made it clear that whoever said "don't sweat the small stuff" had it right.

The week before my mom went to Florida, I was in an automobile accident that totaled my car – on Christmas Eve.

Fortunately, I was not seriously hurt – not a scratch on me, though I had some bruises.

Was I upset that my car, which I loved, was destroyed?

No, because after all, it's just a car.

I have no doubt that some other people had car accidents that same evening were seriously injured and others were killed.

So complaining over the demise of a 2008 Prius seems to me rather silly.

Not being a natural Pollyanna, I feel funny saying this, but it's true: any day you wake up healthy, with food to eat and roof over your head in a house with working heat, is a good day.

I close with this Scottish proverb quoted by David Ogilvy: "Be happy while you're living, for you're a long time dead."

CHAPTER 17

Why Copywriters Should Never be Arrogant

It mystifies me how it has come to pass that so many copywriters – and other marketers whose success hinges on great copy – have huge egos.

After all, copywriting is one of the most humbling professions I can think of.

My colleague BC explains it this way:

"So many times I have put together a campaign, launched it, and sat back and said 'work, damn it, WORK' – and it did not. Very humbling.

"And by the same token, I launched what I thought was watered down drivel – and saw it pull like gangbusters."

Any copywriter who says every campaign is a winner and claims he has never had any losers is either a liar, or putting out very little work, or not swinging for the fences to beat strong controls.

Once, I mentioned to a big-name client that I thought their top go-to copywriter, a famous freelancer, was great.

She snorted derisively and said, "He has more losers for us than I can count."

Another big-name client confided in me that a legendary copywriter they used wrote 7 promotions in a row that bombed for them.

Once, my client PN called me and said, "You want a laugh?"

On my recommendation, PN had called Mr. X, a famous copywriter, because PN's company had way too much work for me to handle alone.

"I asked the guy what percentage of his promotions were winners," PN told me. "You know what he said? 100%! Ha! I sure hung up the phone fast!"

Another famous copywriter wrote a package for a new client that was so brilliant and creative, the client began recommending the writer to all his cronies.

Then weeks passed, until one day, the famous copywriter got a phone call from the client who said abruptly: "Remember that package you did for me? Total bomb. Didn't work."

The copywriter was stunned ... and the referrals all dried up.

By the way, all of the copywriters I am talking about here are actually tops in the field.

The point is that even the best copywriters don't write winners every time.

Like Mr. X, any copywriter who says every single one of his promotions is a home run is a liar.

And given that even the best copywriters write many packages that bomb during their careers, it is a mystery to me why so many copywriters have huge egos.

If anything, being a copywriter is a humbling profession.

One day you can be king of the world, and the next week you sit there eating humble pie.

And that's the way it is, despite all the bragging you read by copywriters on Facebook and elsewhere to the contrary.

CHAPTER 18

Know What You're Talking About

Recently, I sent an e-mail marketing message to my list offering one of my audio home study programs.

BP, a subscriber of mine whom I like and respect, was highly critical of this offer.

In BP's opinion, "An audio course is reminiscent of platform shoes, the IBM Personal Computer, and when the Bee Gees were all living" – implying that audio products are somehow old school and antiquated.

A simple Google search would in an instant shown BP that his claim of audio being old hat is completely wrong.

According to the Audio Publishers Association (APA), audiobook sales in 2015 totaled more than $1.77 billion, up nearly 21% over 2014.

Also in 2015, 9,630 more audiobook titles were published than in the previous year – bringing the number of audiobooks published in 2015 up to 35,574.

I can also speak a bit from personal experience, not just third-party Google research.

In my tiny online business, CTC Publishing, we have grossed hundreds of thousands of dollars selling how-to information on audio.

The take-aways from BP's brash, subjective, and uninformed claim of audio information obsolescence:

1—Google makes it so quick and easy to do some research, take a few minutes to get the facts before writing or speaking on a topic.

2—Don't give subjective opinions on topics that have factual and undisputable answers. Want to debate about whether Trump will be a good president? Feel free. Want to argue that Theresa Caputo can speak to the dead? That's a tougher position to defend, given there is no scientific evidence supporting the existence of the afterlife.

3—Don't defend so many of your positions so rapidly and vehemently. We are not always right. We are often wrong.

In his best-selling Spencer novels, the late Robert B. Parker said of Spender's sidekick Haw: "Hawk always knows what he is talking about. Not because he knows everything. But because he only talks about things he knows."

Good advice for every human being on Earth, in my opinion.

CHAPTER 19

The Return to Old School Media for Learning and Fun

In an article in The New York Review of Books (2/9/2017), Bill McKibben notes that an increasing number of folks are turning away from electronic communication and instead choosing old-school media. For instance:

>> In 2006, just 900,000 new vinyl records were sold in the U.S. In 2015, the number of vinyl records sold was 23 million – an increase of 20% per year.

>> Despite a hefty $150 price for an annual subscription, in the last decade the magazine The Economist has seen its print circulation grow by 600,000.

>> Students who take massive open online courses (MOOCs) perform worse, and learn less, than their peers who are sitting in a school listening to a teacher talking in front of a blackboard.

>> In many classrooms and office conference rooms, schools and corporations are replacing digital smartboards with paper and colored markers.

>> Hundreds of board game parlors, where people get together to play on game boards made of cardboard moving pieces made of plastic or metal, have opened in North America.

So ... what are the reasons a portion of the population is turning back to old media?

>> Well, in the case of records, people enjoy handling and playing them, and appreciate the cover art and liner notes. They also gain a sense of ownership over the music some don't get from digital.

>> For The Economist, when you carry the print edition, people can see what you are reading, which if the magazine is prestigious, shows you are smart, cultured, and in-the-know. Much harder to see that the bloke next to you is reading The Economist without sticking your face right in front of his smart phone.

>> MOOCs does not surprise me. Podcasts, online courses, streaming video, and other digital classes simply cannot match the interaction and personalized attention a teacher gives in a classroom or a speaker like me gives at a live workshop.

>> As for video games vs. board games, McKibben quotes writer David Sax: "Even if you were playing World of Warcraft with the same group of friends around the world each day, talking smack over your headsets, and typing in snippets of conversation, you were ultimately alone in a room with a screen, and the loneliness washed over you like a wave when the game ended."

Another problem with social media in particular is that it may be hazardous to your mental health: One study, reported in Investopedia, concludes that the more often Facebook users click "Like," click on others' posts, or update their own status, the more likely they are to suffer mental health problems in the future. Other studies found that feelings of isolation, anxiety, and inadequacy appeared to rise with increased social media usage.

CHAPTER 20

Seven Graphic Design Tips to Boost Response

Last week I asked ace graphic designer Dwight Ingram for some ideas on how to improve the performance of our direct mail and online marketing through changes in design.

Dwight replied:

"Sometimes it's the little things that make the biggest difference. I'm often called upon to 'freshen up' a fatiguing control, and I've developed a toolkit of small design changes that can revitalize a promotion without having to create a whole new piece."

Here are 7 of Dwight's go-to design tips you can use to boost response and breathe new life into your control:

1—Change the envelope or the outside of the mail piece. If the design is too busy, remove, or move something. If the design is too simple, add something.

Try a new teaser, freshen up the design, and try new fonts. Use the back... think of the extra space like a buck slip. It's a great place to showcase the product and reinforce the offer.

2—Use bigger buttons. For e-mails and landing pages, try a bigger button, a different color, or change the shape. Add a button to the top or bottom in a key location near the offer language.

3–Simplify. Try to make the order process clean and fast especially in digital efforts. Don't make your audience jump through hoops to order.

One of the first things to look at is how many fields are on a form? Are there too many choices, and is the process intuitive? Decide what information you must ask for and what you can eliminate.

4–Change the order form. Enhance the format of your form by adding a notch, or make it an L-shape. Strengthen your offer language, focus on the key benefits. Add an offer summary box. Stress the deadline. Use more personalization, but not too much, and use it appropriately!

5–Add an insert. A lift note, buck slip, or other insert can focus your prospect on the right features or benefits of the product. Highlight the guarantee, the premium, or a unique feature of your product or service.

6–If you use a business reply envelope (BRE), change the color. Using a different paper color for the BRE can lift response by reinforcing the need to respond, but it also adds to the cost, so do the math, and test.

7–Make sure your e-mails, landing pages, and order pages are coded to display optimally not only on PCs but on every other device including tablets and smart phones. (I'll have an entire chapter on designing e-mails for smart phones in my forthcoming book "The Ultimate E-Mail Handbook" from Skyhorse Publishing.)

Remember, it's all about clarity and thinking like a potential customer. If your offer is hidden, or too complicated, or if you're asking for too much information, your response will be affected. Make it easy.

Shameless plug: Dwight Ingram is Owner and Creative Director at Ingram Creative Services. He can be reached by e-mail at <u>dwight@ingramcs.com</u>, or by phone, 919-265-8605.

CHAPTER 21

Why I Hate Cold Calling

My dear, departed friend, marketing consultant Pete Silver, formulated what he called the Silver Rule of Marketing.

The Silver Rule of Marketing says: it is better to get prospects to come to you, rather than you going to them.

Cold calling is at the bottom of my list of marketing channels to use because it violates the Silver Rule of Marketing.

It also puts you at a disadvantage because of the "Busy Doctor Syndrome," described by the late consultant Howard Shenson decades ago.

Howard observed that prospects would rather to a doctor who seems busy and successful, rather than one with an empty waiting room and schedule.

When you cold call to sell your own services, you violate both of these maxims.

First, cold calling by definition means you, the seller, are going to them, the prospects – rather than the prospects coming to you, as it should be ... a clear violation of the Silver Rule.

Second, cold calling to pitch your own services destroys any possibility of you being the Busy Doctor.

After all, if you were really busy, you would have no time to cold call, because you'd be inundated with work and deadlines.

Cold calling can work in some situations, but it's absolutely at the bottom of the barrel for any freelance or self-employed professional selling his or her own services.

Some cold calls actually disguise their voice, create a second persona, and pretend to be somebody else doing the cold call for the service provider.

It can work, but it's starting off the relationship on a deception.

Better is to have staff or hire an independent sales reps to make the cold calls, establish a relationship, and then pass qualified leads on to you.

This way you almost never speak to unqualified prospects, which saves you an enormous amount of time.

What do I do personally for my copywriting business? No cold calls. I use the Silver Rule, which is to do marketing that gets prospects to come to me, rather than the other way around.

I've covered this in detail in several of my books including "Secrets of a Freelance Writer" (Henry Holt) and "Become a Recognized Authority in Your Field" (Alpha), both available used for a few bucks on www.amazon.com.

CHAPTER 22

What Einstein Missed About Relativity

A kindly subscriber sent me a generous gift: a beautiful hardcover copy of Stephen Hawking's best-selling book "A Brief History of Time."

I am now reading it, though slowly, as I find many of the concepts difficult to wrap my mind around.

But here's one thing about time that Hawking missed in his book about time. Einstein also missed it in his book "Relativity: the Special and General Theory."

Namely, the older we get, the faster time goes. That's Bly's Theory of Relativity!

Conversely, the younger we are, the more slowly times passes.

When you are 5 and your 6th birthday is a month away, that month feels like forever.

When you are 12, the 4 or 5 years you must wait to get your driver's license seems like an eternity.

And as much as I liked college – and I did, for the most part – it seemed to me at times during my 4 years as an undergraduate that I would be there forever.

But now, I will soon turn 60 – and yet, it seems to me I was just 21 ... and starting my first corporate job at Westinghouse ... only yesterday.

My sons recently turned 27 and 24 – and they have reached that age in the blink of an eye.

Life itself goes by in a flash – and the older you get, the faster it moves.

Also as we age, our opportunities and options become fewer and fewer – a statement I know some of you will dispute, but hey, I calls them as I sees them!

When I was 21, for instance, I briefly considered going back to school to become a pediatrician – and I believe I could have done so.

For me now, at 60, medical school and a residency are clearly off the table.

I don't know if any of this is helpful, but I can tell you my 3 guidelines for making the most of each day while you are still alive:

1–Every day, without fail, tell your spouse and your children (and grandchildren, if you have them, which I do not) that you love them. Every day. Even if they complain that you say it too much.

2–Be kind and generous to others. Do not exert power or show meanness or cruelty, especially to those weaker than you. Remember, just because you can do something to someone doesn'tmean you SHOULD do it to them.

3–Find work you enjoy. Get good at it and keep at it. A career, job, or profession you love can give you happiness every day. As Max Ehrmann wrote in Desiderata: "Keep interested in your own career, however humble, it's a real possession in the changing fortunes of time."

The expression "tempus fugit" – time flies – is true. In an interview, Barbara Walters once asked Isaac Asimov, "What would you do if you had only 6 months to live."

"Type faster," he said, without missing a beat.

CHAPTER 23

Sloppy Spelling in the Internet Age

Subscriber TW writes:

"Bob, here's a question I'd love to see you address in one of your e-mails: Have you noticed the constant misspellings and incorrect homonyms on the Web and in e-mails? People not knowing the difference between 'to,' 'two,' and 'too' – or 'there' and 'their'? Terrible grammar?

"Did you think that the ability to dictate on smartphones and other devices and our reliance on spellcheck and text shorthand (" r u home?") is dumbing us down? Either that or is it desensitizing us to these types of errors?"

Well, we have always lived with spelling and grammar mistakes – but yes, they have definitely increased in e-mail and on Websites. What's the reason for the proliferation of typos online?

In e-mail, it's two things.

First, people are crushingly busy today. So they dash off their e-mails as fast as they can, without reading them over or even using the e-mail proofing function.

Second, some people believe that e-mails don't have to be as flawless as a traditional letter. And so they are sloppy e-mail writers.

Unfortunately, many of their e-mail readers are aghast when they see bad grammar and spelling errors. As a result, such mistakes distract your readers, diverting attention to the typos and away from the content of the message.

Some readers even lower their opinion of you and what you are saying if there is even a single misspelling.

As for Web content, there are also two reasons for the proliferation of spelling and grammar mistakes in Web pages, white papers, blogs, and other online writing.

First, back in the day, before the Internet, when our writing was all print, we proofread carefully, because if an error was found after a magazine article, direct mail letter, or product brochure was printed, it would cost a fortune to go back to press. So we were much more careful.

Today, if you write and post a new Web page, and someone spots a typos, it can be corrected literally in minutes at virtually zero cost. Easy peasy, no biggie.

Second, with large Websites having dozens or hundreds of pages, many of the pages come from different sources – product pages, articles, blogs, press releases, newsletters – some of which were created for other purposes and then posted on the site.

So many firms just either don't have or are not willing to devote the time to carefully proofing each new page.

It's not that they don't think proofreading is important, but rather it is not at the top of their priority list, and they do not have the bandwidth or resources to get to it.

Back in the day, when I did a lot of corporate training seminars, I took great pains to make sure my workbooks were error-free.

But the occasional typo or grammatical error still crept in from time to time.

And because I was often teaching writing, that made me look bad.

So I turned it into a game.

At the beginning of the workshop, I took a roll of quarters out of my pocket and slammed it on the lectern.

I then told the class I'd pay them to "proof" their workbook – and pay a quarter to the person who brought a typo to my attention.

This took away the stigma of spelling mistakes, turned it into a fun game, and actually got them to pay more attention to the workbook.

The most it ever cost me at a full-day seminar was 75 cents.

They learned. Had fun. And I got my proofreading for pennies on the dollar!

CHAPTER 24

Why I Personally Answer E-mails and Questions from My Subscribers

I get a lot of e-mail from subscribers.

And even though it's time-consuming, I respond to as many as I can – which is most.

Why?

I believe that when you make your e-mail marketing a two-way communication, you build a stronger relationship with your subscribers.

The result: greater engagement, more readership, and increased sales when you offer your list a product they might like.

A week or so ago subscriber JI sent me this brief e-mail:

"I enjoyed your article today. I like the way you communicate what you believe and how you respond to people.

"At the same time, I see that I can leave a conversation with you while taking away my own view of life without hurting your feelings.

"It's nice getting to know you over these years and I do love you as a person for what you are giving the world. Thank you."

I know from publishing The Direct Response Letter for more than a dozen years that, like JI, many of my subscribers appreciate that I am accessible – both via e-mail, Facebook, and phone.

Conversely, I have heard many say they dislike it when they write to the publishers of their favorite e-newsletters, and all they get in return is an impersonal auto-responder message – many of which say the author cannot respond personally.

Maybe I am stupid to maintain a dialogue with my subscribers – Lord knows I'm busy enough.

But I do it for three primary reasons:

>> First, I think if you have a question or comment, you deserve a personal response from me.

>> Second, I enjoy hearing from and talking with my readers. Some reach out to me only once in a blue moon. Others are regulars. I like both.

>> Third, it lets me know what you are interested in, so I can produce content that is useful and relevant to you.

I believe the give-and-take interaction between an editor and his subscribers enhances the experienced of getting the e-newsletter for readers and adds value.

So I plan to continue it for many both the immediate and long-term future.

And thanks for reading my e-mail essays. It's much appreciated.

By the way, about once a year I collect what readers and I think are the best of the essays, and publish them both as a Kindle e-book and a Create Space paperback.

These essay collections typically run 200 to 240 pages or so and contain 75 to 85 essays.

Here's the most recent:

https://www.amazon.com/Blys-Little-Blue-Business-Wisdom/dp/1539100081/ref=sr_1_1?s=books&ie=UTF8&qid=1486683951&sr=1-1&keywords=Bob+bly%27s+little+blue+book+of+business+wisdom

Mary Ellen Tribby writes, "It's amazing, every time Bob writes a book I learn something useful I can apply to my business immediately.

"Well he has done it again with LITTLE BLUE BOOK OF BUSINESS WISDOM. Only this time, not only is there great business advice, this book it is ALSO filled with life advice.

"Oh as an added bonus, it will make you laugh. I recommend you read it cover to cover, I did!"

CHAPTER 25

How Many Rewrites Should You Do?

Subscriber RL sent me this comment from the late suspense novelist Robert B. Parker—one of my favorite commercial authors:

"I do first draft. I don't revise. I don't reread. I send it in. They edit it. But they don't make any significant changes."

By comparison, Hemingway revised every morning. He claimed to have written one of the pages of "A Farewell to Arms" 59 times.

George Plimpton asked him why. Was there some technical problem? What was so hard?

Hemingway replied: "Getting the words right."

And poet Donald Hall said he rewrote one of his poems 600 times.

The problem is this.....

For most of us, if we don't revise and rewrite enough, our writing is not as good as it could be.

On the other hand, if we do endless rewrites and edits, the piece never gets finished – and if we are working on a flat project fee, we end up making less than minimum wage.

To answer this question about the ideal number of rewrites, I made a short video on the subject of "How many rewrites should you do before you consider the piece finished."

You can watch it free here:

https://www.youtube.com/watch?v=MvJYB4BnT48&t=6s

I agree with actor Michael J. Fox, who said, "Strive for excellence, not perfection."

CHAPTER 26

The Power of the Double Pipeline

Subscriber DC writes:

"I've been a full-time freelance copywriter for 21 years. It's been great — but maintaining a constant flow of good projects has been harder work than I ever imagined.

"I know this is 'feast or famine', but it requires massive effort to overcome. Many business books (certainly not yours) gloss over this fact.

"Some books on freelancing show pictures of freelancers with laptops on the beach. In my experience, nothing could be further from the truth!

"There's freelancing myth and hype — and freelancing reality.

"I love being a freelance copywriter; at 51 I'm a 'veteran' and I can't imagine doing anything else.

"But it requires constant marketing and effort — more now than ever — which you rightly emphasize in your books."

DC speculates the vast majority of freelance copywriters are not as busy as they would like — even though 95% won't admit it.

So, how do you escape the "feast or famine" cycle — and stay busy and profitable all year long?

The answer is my "double pipeline" method. It works as follows:

First, figure out how much marketing you have to do to generate enough work to meet your income goal.

As an example, assume Joe, a copywriter, generates his leads primarily via direct mail.

His income goal is $100,000 gross revenue a year. His average job pays $2,000 per assignment.

Joe works 50 weeks a year, so he needs one $2,000 job per week to hit his $100,000 sales target,

Now, say his direct mail package generates a 3% response rate, and he closes one out of every three leads on average.

If Joe sent out 100 mailers a week, this would yield 3 inquiries and one paid assignment, meeting his income goal of $2,000 a week.

So 100 mailers a week keeps Joe's lead pipeline full.

But my "double pipeline" methods says you should calculate how much marketing and self-promotion it would take to meet your sales goal.

Then do DOUBLE that amount of marketing. If Joe's calculations shows he needs to send 100 sales letters a week to meet his income goal, he should send 200 letters a week.

That way, his pipeline will not merely have enough leads to generate the work he needs. It will have twice the volume of inquiries required to generate the 100K in revenues he wants.

Of course, thanks to referrals, repeat business, and other sources of leads – social media, blogging, and what have you – Joe realistically won't need to send 200 or maybe even 100 mailers weekly.

But the point of the "double pipeline" methods is this: doing more marketing and self-promotion than you need to gives you an abundance of leads – more than you need.

Having the doubly full lead pipeline is your protection against slow times and virtually assures that you are busy, productive, and profitable all year long.

Try doubling up in your marketing, and fill your lead pipeline to overflowing. It's your insurance against an unwanted slowdown in leads and work.

CHAPTER 27

Why I Hate Telemarketing

As a marketer, I am supposed to be open to using whatever marketing channel will work for me and my clients.

But extreme distaste makes me avoid one – and only one – marketing method: outbound telemarketing to cold lists.

There are three reasons why I believe I can always find a better – read: more effective and less offensive – method than outbound telemarketing to cold lists.

First, when predictive dialers are used, there is a time delay between the prospect answering the phone and the start of the conversation.

This wastes the prospect's time and annoys her in a way that, to me, is unacceptable.

Second, people are so much busier today, your call is almost always an unwelcome interruption.

At work I have to inform the telemarketer that I am on a deadline and therefore cannot talk with him.

At home, the telemarketer is interrupting a meal, family time, or leisure time – none of which is welcome.

Third, more than half of the telemarketers who call me today have thick regional, ethnic, or nation-specific accents.

The accents are so strong that I literally cannot understand what they are saying.

This forces me to ask them to repeat what they just said multiple times if I want to continue the conversation – which I don't.

And don't even get me started on outright scams, like the guy who called yesterday.

He said he was from Microsoft, had detected a problem with my PC software, and I needed to give him remote access to my computer to fix it.

My friend BC has a great comeback for this scam: He tells the telemarketer, "I don't have a computer." If someone asks for his credit card, he says "I don't have a credit card." Smart!

About once a week, someone says they are calling about my utility bill from Jersey Central Power and Light.

And when I get them to admit they not with JCP&L, I tell them, "Well, then we have no reason to discuss my bill." That only gets them talking faster, and I immediately hang up.

The day before, I got another common scam call: a young man who said, when I answered the phone, "Grandpa, I need your help."

I am amazed this works on some people, and how could it work on me, given I do not have grandkids?

But then again, I know someone who actually sent a check for $10,000 to get unclaimed funds from a scam artist in Nigeria.

Also, when you pick up the phone and a recorded voice says, "This is an urgent public service announcement" – trust me, it isn't.

Subscriber PA add:

"In 1969 I tried a radical approach to getting new subscribers for our local newspaper. I hired 6 people to call the folks in town.

"Our call list was pages torn from the phone book's white pages. Our auto-dialer was the eraser end of pencils, because those rotary dials were tough on fingernails.

"First, I hired housewives who were thrilled with the chance to talk to people. They talked a lot, but not always about the newspaper. Then I hired students from the debate team at the local college. They argued with people.

"I shut it down after 6 months. We had alienated more people than we signed up.

"It was a bad idea nearly 50 years ago and it's still a bad idea today."

I guess you can't go broke underestimating the intelligence of the American public, and certain telemarketers and spammers seem to be leading the movement to make as much fraudulent profit from us as possible.

CHAPTER 28

SEO for White Papers

Want to help more search engine users find your white paper?

My esteemed colleague, white paper guru Gordon Graham, recently told me and his many other readers that, just like a Web page, your white papers should be optimized for search engines.

As Gordon explained, "Web spiders can index PDFs on the Web so that they show up in search results."

That's why you should always include your chosen keywords as "descriptive metadata" in any white paper you post online.

(Descriptive metadata can include elements such as title, abstract, author, and keywords.)

So how do you insert the metadata with the keywords into your white paper PDF?

To insert metadata using Adobe Acrobat:

1. Open the PDF with Acrobat and select File > Properties.

2. In the Document Properties dialog, on the Description panel, enter your preferred title, author, subject, and keywords (separated by commas) in the appropriate text boxes. Then click OK.

3. Select File > Save.

To insert metadata using InDesign:

If you have InDesign, you can insert metadata in your white paper file and then generate a fresh PDF.

If your designers don't know how to do this, share the following process with them:

1. Open the white paper file with InDesign and select File > File Info.

2. In the File Info dialog box, enter your preferred document title, author, description, and keywords (separated by commas) in the appropriate text boxes. Then click OK.

3. Select File > Save to save your updated file.

4. Then select File > Export.

5. In the Export dialog, select Adobe PDF with your regular PDF options. Then click OK.

To insert metadata using Word:

If you have a recent version of Word, you can insert metadata in a more roundabout way. Here's how:

1. Open the white paper file with Word, press Alt+F, and select Prepare > Properties.

2. In the Document Information panel, enter your preferred title, subject, and keywords (separated by commas) in the appropriate text boxes.

3. Press Alt+F and select Save As and then select PDF or XPS.

4. In the Publish as PDF or XPS dialog, navigate to the folder you want, enter a suitable file name, and click Publish.

To insert metadata using your Mac:

If you have a Mac, you can use Adobe Acrobat or InDesign as described earlier.

Or you can use a nifty piece of freeware that makes up for the limitations of Preview, called Combine PDFs. You can download it here:

http://monkeybreadsoftware.de/Freeware/CombinePDFs.shtml

When you have Combine PDFs running, do this:

1. Select File > Add Files.

2. In the Open dialog, select the white paper PDF and click Open, then select Options > Add Metadata.

3. In the Add Metadata dialog, enter your preferred title, author, subject, and keywords (separated by commas). Then click OK.

4. Click Merge PDFs in the lower-right corner.

5. In the Save dialog, enter a file name and click Save.

Note that CombinePDFs is shareware, so after you process 1,000 pages with it, it asks you to pay for a license.

Gordon advises that if you use it that much, you should shell out for it.

CHAPTER 29

Writing Message from a Cheesy Horror Movie

While channel surfing, I came across a horror movie, and the description at the bottom of the screen read:

"Stranded in the countryside, a monstrous scarecrow terrorizes a group of teens."

This is one of the most common grammar mistakes, and it is called a dangling participle or dangling modifier.

The first part of the sentence – "stranded in the countryside" – modifies or describes a noun in the second part of the sentence.

The rules of grammar require that the noun being modified be closer to the modifier phrase than any other part of the sentence.

In this example, it is obviously the teens who are stranded and being terrorized by the scarecrow.

We know this because if the teens were not stranded, they could just leave and avoid the monster.

The monster, being able to talk and teleport, was certainly NOT stranded.

The sentence should read: "Stranded in the countryside, a group of teens is terrorized by a monstrous scarecrow."

The dangling modifier is a common mistake in the lead paragraph of business letters.

For instance, here is the opening of a letter written by a sales rep for an inventory control software system mailed to warehouse managers.

It begins, "As a warehouse manager, I know inventory control is critical to your success."

This is wrong because it says the letter writer – "I" – is a warehouse manager, which he is not.

The correct grammar would be: "As a warehouse manager, you know that inventory control is critical to your success."

CHAPTER 30

The Awful Truth About Self-Publishing

Whenever I mention that I prefer traditional publishing to self-publishing, two things happen.

First, I get a slew of e-mails from writers telling me traditional publishing is awful – low advances, low royalties, and publishers not promoting their books.

Second, I get another flood of e-mails from authors telling me that they or other self-publishers are "crushing it," making money hand over fist.

They often cite Amanda Hocking, who has sales of over $2.5 million for her self-published Kindle e-book.

But according to a survey of 1,007 self-publishing authors by the Website Taleist, conducted by Dave Cornford and Steven Lewis in 2011 (yes, it's a bit dated), the truth is quite different.

"The majority of the information out there is about the outliers, whose success is inspiring, but as we can now confirm bears scant resemblance to the experience of most authors," said Dave Cornford and Steven Lewis.

According to their survey, half of self-published authors make less than $500 a year.

That's because, as reported in a 2015 article by Chris McMullen, the average self-published book sells less than 250 copies.

Derek Murphy, an expert in independent publishing, says, "The average self-published author spends $2,000 to $5,000 to publish their books, and few earn any money."

If you spend two grand and sell 250 copies, you are losing a lot of money on your self-published book!

By comparison, in traditional publishing, the money flows from publisher to author, even though advances are much smaller today than when I started writing books 25 years ago.

The mainstream publishers not only give you money up front; they also pay for everything, from printing and cover design to editing and proofreading – saving you a considerable amount of cash.

The bell curve for self-publishing is skewed, with less than 10% of self-published authors earning about three-quarters of the total revenues from sales of self-published books.

The average self-publisher from the group surveyed by Taleist earns just $10,000 a year.

Notice also that many self-publishers with good sales, from El James ("Fifty Shades of Grey"), Robert Ringer ("Looking Out for #1"), and Roger von Oech ("A Whack on the Side of the Head") either immediately or eventually look for and get a deal with a mainstream publishing house.

Take note: I am not saying mainstream publishing is great or the better way to go.

My purpose here is to just present some cold, hard facts for all those self-publishing cheerleaders I constantly hear from to ponder – and to inform the rest of us about the good, the bad, and the ugly of being your own publisher.

CHAPTER 31

What Does Your Office Say About You

What can you tell about a person by the way he decorates his office?

In my case, I look around and immediately see the following:

1–A fax machine. People tell me fax is old technology. I wouldn't give mine up; I even maintain a dedicated phone line.

2–A gigantic wall poster of about two dozen of the major Marvel superheroes.

3–A small abstract oil painting by my friend and sometimes coauthor Gary Blake.

4–A framed picture of my two sons when they were young. Press a button on the frame and it plays a message they recorded for me around when the picture was taken!

5–Many other photos of my kids all over the walls.

6–Several toy robots including Robbie the Robot from Forbidden Planet and Robot B-9 from Lost in Space.

7–My two favorite coffee mugs, one that says "I'm a chemical engineer – just like a regular guy, only smarter" ... and the second which reads, "My story begins in Paterson, NJ."

8–A picture of my little sister and me when we were very young, holding hands.

9–A picture of Stan Lee, personally autographed and made out to me and my boys – a gift from copywriter Peter Fogel.

10–A scale model of a 1962 Chevy Belair, the car my father bought new when I was 5. He died 22 years ago when I was 37, so it has great sentimental meaning to me.

11–A framed certificate recognizing me as a member of the American Institute of Chemical Engineers since 1979. Why? It's beautiful certificate, nicer-looking than my college diploma, which hangs directly below it.

12–A handsome Successories desk clock with a transparent center through which you can see the faux gears (the clock runs on a battery). Also a gift.

13–A cabinet and rack with dozens of assorted CDs – mostly rock, jazz, classical, and pop – from Madonna and Elvis, to Maynard Ferguson and Beethoven.

14–A poster of Grumpy Cat that says "Go Away."

15–A desk lamp that simulates the wavelength of natural sunlight. It is supposed to make one less grumpy. I have no idea if it affects my mood one way or the other, though I suspect not.

16–Oddly, only a very few reference books. Reason: I need the shelves in my office bookcases for three-ring binders, which hold the background materials for each of my current projects and recent. I have plenty of bookcases in other nearby rooms holding my other books. No need to clutter my limited workspace with them.

17–My desk faces a window overlooking our one-acre heavily wooded back yard. Almost every day I see a small herd of deer march past the window.

18–I had a fishbowl with a beta fish I got as a gift, but it was too small. So I got him a tank with proper lighting and filtration. But I was out of space in the office so he's now across the hall. I miss looking at the little guy!

19–I have two 4-drawer metal file cabinets that hold hanging file folders – and a few steps away, down in a large finished room in our basement, 9 more just l like them.

20–I have a framed Mark Alan Stamaty poster with a slightly mocking cartoon of how Madison Avenue advertising agencies work – a gift from the Village Voice given back in the day when I was an advertising manager who bought ad space.

My dirty little secret: all of these add up to a strangely warm, familiar, and comforting environment in which I MUST be to do my work.

I am in awe of you who are able to work productively anywhere outside of your home office – on a plane, at the beach, in a hotel room, Starbucks.

I just can't do it. Nor do I want to. Since I love to work and can only do so at maximum output in my home office, the result is I am here 12 hours a day, despise travel, and seldom go anywhere.

So … what's in your office that you treasure … that you like … and that would tell me something about who you are or what you like?

By the way, I am going to rearrange some things to get the beta back in the office in his new tank and also add either a small terrarium or a few succulents and cacti.

CHAPTER 32

What David McCullough Can Teach You About Hard Work

In an interview with the Harvard Business Review, the then 79-year-old (now 83) Pulitzer-Prize-winning historian David McCullough explained why he had no intention of retiring from writing.

"I'm having a ball. I can't wait to get out of bed every morning. To me, it's the only way to live.

"When the founders wrote about life, liberty, and the pursuit of happiness, they didn't mean longer vacations and more comfortable hammocks. They meant the pursuit of learning. The love of learning. The pursuit of improvement and excellence.

"I keep telling students, Find work you love. Don't concern yourself overly about how much money is involved or whether you're ever going to be famous.

I'm giving a talk at Dartmouth this week. It's called the Hard Work of Writing. And it is hard work. But in hard work is happiness."

However, there's a flaw in David's hard work equals happiness equation.

Namely, if you actually like or love the work you do, then hard work will indeed make you happy.

Conversely, if you work 9 to 5, forty hours a week at a job that either bores you or you actively dislike – or even hate – the result is the opposite of happiness.

You feel like a prisoner or indented slave, stuck seemingly forever in a rut. And as my late client SK once observed, "A rut is a grave without a cover."

To me the 4 most important things in my life are (a) my family, (b) our health, (c) having enough money that we are financially secure, and (d) having work I don't just like but absolutely love.

So I place a bit more emphasis on money than McCullough. Reason: If you struggle to buy groceries or pay the rent, money worries can take over your life, making you unable to enjoy your days to the fullest.

Fortunately, I more or less have most of those items on the list. I was recently in a car crash, which endangered item B for me, but after just 4 weeks of physical therapy, I was 100% recovered.

I can't exactly articulate why I love reading and writing so much – I just do. I have written since the 7th grace, and now, as I will be 60 in July, there is still nothing I would rather do.

I have other interests. I have a few hobbies. My wife and I socialize with friends. But that's peripheral for me.

If I can write 10 to 12 hours a day, working on projects that interest me – and I am careful to take on only those writing projects that do – and then read after work, I am a happy camper.

As for my main leisure activity, I want to do less around the house, so I have given up my lifelong hobby of keeping freshwater and saltwater aquariums as well as terrariums.

My kids and I have had everything from blue lobsters (actually blue crayfish), Oscars, eels, turtles, and a stingray. Fun while it lasted, but I no longer want to keep tanks. All that's left is a 5-gallone plastic tank with a beta fish.

And I am not totally without hobbies: In addition to reading, I play the clarinet.

CHAPTER 33

Charles Bukowski on Writing and Rewriting

A lot of people are complainers and whiners.

We copywriters are no exception.

One of the most common complaints I hear from copywriter centers around clients requesting edits and changes.

But the great novelist and poet, Charles Bukowski, had a more positive take on rewrites.

In his book "On Writing" (Ecco, 2015, p. 163), Bukowski writes:

"Writing has never been work to me, and even when it comes out badly, I like the action, the sound of the typer, a way to go.

"And even when I write badly and it comes back, I look at it and I don't mind too much: I've got a chance to improve.

"That's the matter of staying with it, tapping away ... until it sounds and reads and feel better."

Three quick points for freelance copywriters to think about:

1–You may know more about copywriting than your client. But he may know more about his market than you – and almost certainly knows more about his product than you.

2–You will have some clients who know as much or even more about copywriting than you do. You know who they are. Writing for these clients takes your skills to the next level.

Once, when my client MF, one of the masters of copywriting, was reviewing a draft of mine, his comments were all so on target I was moved to say aloud, "I am learning so much – I should be paying YOU."

He wryly replied: "You're damned right."

3–We don't always write as well as we would like to. But we must always write as well as we can.

Of course, it helps if you – like Charles Bukowski, Isaac Asimov, and David McCullough – belong to the segment of writers who not only like but actually love to write.

"There is nothing more magic than lines forming across paper," said Bukowski. "It's all there. It's all there ever was. What comes afterwards is more than secondary.

"I can't understand any writer who stops writing. It's like taking your heart out and flushing it away. I'll write to my last breath. I was meant to be like this.

"And when my skeleton rests upon the bottom of the casket, nothing will be able to subtract from these splendid nights, sitting here at this machine."

Bukowski's words remind me of when Barbara Walters interviewed Isaac Asimov.

She asked Asimov, "What would you do if you found out you had only 6 months to live?"

Without missing a beat, Asimov replied: "I'd type faster."

My kind of guys....

P.S. I also think some young marketers who, in this digital age, think they know it all, should heed this observation from Bukowski: "Youth has something about it that makes you think you are much better than you are."

CHAPTER 34

The Most Powerful Time Management Technique Ever Devised

Your most valuable resource is not money. You can always get more money.

It is time. Time is irreplaceable. When it is gone, you can't get it back. And your supply is severely limited.

I am not telling you something you do not already know.

So the way I am going to help you today is to give you my most powerful strategy for using your time wisely and efficiently.

It is: outsourcing.

Simply put, this means doing only those things that, in the words of info marketing guru Fred Gleeck, "make the highest and best use of your time."

About the only 2 things I devoted my life to – and spent all my time on – were writing and being the best father I could be.

Those are the highest and best use of my time, because they delivered the most value to me, my clients, my publishers, my readers, and my family.

When you focus on the things that matter most and jettison the rest, you save time, make more money, and have a happier and more enjoyable life.

Here are just a few of the things that other people do themselves but I rarely or never do myself and instead outsource to others:

>> Lawn care – a total waste of my time. I hire a service to mow the grass, trim the bushes, and pick up the leaves.

>> Snow shoveling – another waste of time. I have a service on call to plow and shovel us whenever it snows.

>> Accounting and bookkeeping – I have a bookkeeper on staff and outsource tax preparation to a local CPA.

>> House cleaning – we outsource that to a housecleaning service, as I have better things to do with my time than vacuuming or dusting.

>> Home repairs – local plumbers, electricians, contractors, and handymen love us, because they do everything to upkeep our home and its systems.

Why? Most of the work I cannot even do. The work I could do, they do 4 times faster and 4 times better than I could.

And I can spend the time at my computer writing for clients instead, so hiring them as actually a profit center rather than a cost center. It is. Think about it.

>> Building houses for the poor – good works are important. But by earning more money, I have more to give to charitable organizations, essentially "outsourcing" my good works to them.

CHAPTER 35

The Awful Truth About How-To Books

Comedienne Steven Wright famously quipped: "If how-to books really worked, we'd only need just one."

Well, recently I received as a gift a new how-to business book.

In the preface, the author shocked me by stating, "The average person who buys any how-to information gets little or no results."

Do you believe it? From long experience, I certainly do.

And if so, is this dose of realism at the beginning of a new how-to book demotivating, discouraging, a rude awakening, or inspiration to beat the averages ... and be one of those who DO get results?

I have no solid proof of these numbers, but I think they are pretty accurate.

If you sell 10,000 copies of your how-to business book or course, 10% of those who buy – a thousand people – will actually skim or read it.

Of those 1,000 readers, only 10% – just 100 of them – will do some or all of what you recommend in the book.

Finally, of the 100 who actually work your system, most will give up too soon, because it's hard work or they get distracted.

And only 10% – just 10 people – will gain the skill, start the business, and actually make money from it.

As a how-to author, I get the most satisfaction from those 10 buyers who actually follow the advice and get the result they want. They represent just 0.1% of your 10,000 purchasers.

But if I can help even 10 people achieve their business or career goals, I can be happy that at least I have changed their lives for the better.

It does happen. Reader SS writes, "I built a career based on one of your how-to books, Bob. That being said, I've read many how-to books that were very good – yet, I didn't do much with the information. I don't think I'm alone in that."

And JM reports, "I bought the copywriter's handbook 3 years ago from my meager pay. The book paid for itself almost immediately."

In consulting, where clients are paying thousands of dollars for customized advice instead of just $15 to $25 for a book, consultant HB once told me:

"Only half my clients listen to my advice, and of those, they implement only half what I tell them. So 75% of my recommendations are ignored, despite the high fees I charge."

In closing, Steve Wright said, "I went to the bookstore and asked the clerk where the self-help section was."

She replied: "I could show you, but that would defeat the purpose."

CHAPTER 36

To Sell to People, Become More Like Them

I am not a tough guy or a macho man or particularly strong.

But what if that's what you need to be to fit in with your colleagues, customers, or coworkers?

While I was going to college, I worked summers and Christmas breaks in the warehouse of a company that distributed potato chips, pretzels, and other snacks.

It was a minimum wage job, and I was the only college student – and the only employee who worked just seasonally – everyone else in the warehouse was full time.

About two-thirds of the crew were adults stuck in a low-pay, dead-end job; one-third were younger guys about my age who were either high school drop-outs...

...or, if they had graduated, had gone as far as they were going to go in their education. And they all knew I was in college studying chemistry.

Naturally, spending 40 hours a week working side by side with them, I wanted to fit in as best I could.

Well, the toughest guy there was "Big Hank," an incredibly strong forklift operator who stood about 6' 2" and weighed around 300 pounds – almost all of it muscle.

One day, on the lunch break, Hank got into a challenge game with the guys one at a time.

Hank and his opponent would shake hands, and both would squeeze the other's hand as hard as he could – until the victim couldn't take the pain anymore, cried out in agony, and was declared the loser. And Hank never lost.

Worker after worker could not withstand Hank's grip—and begged for release.

After Hank made Chris, the second-strongest guy in the warehouse, yelp in pain and plead with Hank to release his hand, I calmly stepped in front of Hank, looked him in the eye without smiling, and held out my hand – shocking everyone on the crew.

Hank gripped my hand. But no matter how much he squeezed, I stared right back at him, and my expression never changed.

Amazed, he gripped me even harder, and squeezed with all his might, intending to cause me maximum pain – but to no avail.

Finally, realizing he could not beat me, he released his grip, shook his head admiringly, and said out loud, "Fellas, this college boy is the only tough guy in the room aside from me."

Now the truth is, I never tried to squeeze or crush Hank's hand. I was strictly on defense.

And, I have this odd thing in my right hand: no matter how much pressure someone applies, the bones move or slide in such a way that they do not break and I feel virtually no pain.

Hank and the crew did not know that, and so after the contest, they liked me better, because I was more "one of the guys."

The next day, a younger coworker, with whom I was already friendly, wanted to show me his martial arts fighting prowess during lunch.

So he leap off the ground and lashed out at me with a karate kick.

I easily caught his foot in my hands – putting him in an embarrassing positions which amused the onlookers.

To get free, he leapt up to kick me with the other leg, and as that leg went airborne, I released the first leg.

With both legs in the air and nothing to support him, gravity took over and he fell hard on his back and ass – to uproarious laughter aimed at him and some congratulatory pats on the back for me.

I have to admit, these two victories felt kind of good!

Anyway, all the guys became my pals – and on Friday nights we often went to a bar or a pool hall to hang out. I was accepted as part of the gang.

The lesson for you as a marketer is: People like people who are like them.

So the more you can show the prospect that you are "one of his people," the more open and receptive he will be to what you tell him.

One example is that if you are doing direct mail to doctors, you get a better response if the letter appears to be written by and is signed by a doctor.

Same things for lawyers, CPAs, farmers, and construction workers.

Whatever you can do to show the prospect you have something in common with him or her, as long as it is both true and sincere, the better the relationship – and the greater your chance of making a friend ... and the sale.

P.S. Weeks after the Hank test, a couple of the older guys, Lee and Lenny, were giving me a ride home, and as soon as we left the warehouse, they broke out a bottle of VO.

I had never drank whiskey, and they offered me a small cup of it. I took one big gulp and nearly upchucked the contents of my stomach. They had a good laugh, while I grinned sheepishly.

Years later, I tried Dewar's, and discovered that in fact a better brand of Scotch, on the rocks with soda and a twist, was a drink I really enjoyed. I also liked 12-year-old premium Scotch, but with a thin layer of water poured on top.

My violent reaction to the VO did not lower my status in the group, as all the other guys in the warehouse thought VO was crap and chastised Lee and Lenny for drinking the "cheap shit."

CHAPTER 37

Timing is Everything

Amy and I attended a wedding recently.

We knew the parents of the bride but almost no one else there.

Given that I am not outgoing or terribly social, these situations are always uncomfortable for me.

Anyway, to avoid awkward silence, I forced myself to make small talk with the RH, guy sitting next to me at my assigned table.

RH and most of the other friends of the bride's parents, B and M, at the wedding were a tad older than me – early to mid-60s – same age as B and M.

Anyway, I asked RH what he did, and he told me, even though he had been in corporate IT, he was now working as a high school janitor.

I assumed he was fired from his IT position recently.

He was sort of, but not quite.

The company didn't outright fire him.

They said they were shutting down the NJ office near his home where he had worked for over a decade.

They gave him a choice: get downsized or keep your job but move to our NYC office.

"I almost did, but at my age" – RH was 73 when we spoke, but the firing took place over a decade before I met him – "I just didn't want a 90-minute commute to work.

"And so even though I didn't want to leave my job, I refused the offer – and I was out on the street.

"No one wanted to hire an older IT guy whose experience was strictly in older platforms, so I could not get another corporate job and ended up making a tiny fraction of my old salary doing menial work."

But that's not the end of the story.

The company's NYC office was in the World Trade Center.

A few weeks after he would have moved to that office, 911 happened.

Everyone in the office was killed, as RH would have been had he taken the job at the WTC.

The lesson is something you already know.

A lot of what happens in life, good or bad, is timing, which is just a subset of luck.

So don't beat yourself up too much for the bad stuff – and conversely, don't pat yourself on the back too briskly for the good stuff.

Much of what happens results from factors beyond our control.

If you want more proof of this, and see just how factors we have no power determine much of our lives, read Adam Alter's excellent book on that subject, "Drunk Tank Pink" (Penguin).

But here's the good news about timing as it applies to marketing (Alter is a Marketing Professor).

To make the sale, you have to be in front of the prospect at the right time – the time he is ready to consider getting your product.

And the way to be there at the right time is to be there all the time.

In the pre-Internet era, that was almost impossible, because print and broadcast media were generally too expensive for that kind of frequency.

But in the digital age, we *can* be there all the time ... or at least much of the time ... in an affordable way with blogs, e-newsletters, online ads, and other online media.

So timing is everything. And the best way to make sure your timing is right in marketing is to be there all of the time – or as close to that as you can get.

CHAPTER 38

Is College a Waste of Time and Money?

An investment guru I respect recently wrote in his e-newsletter, "It's not necessary to go to college. You're likely to be corrupted, and indebt yourself like an indentured slave for many years to come."

Well, yes, maybe it's not necessary to go to college. But is it a good idea to go?

For many people, yes – and others, no.

Mr. Investment Guru quite correctly points out that the cost of college has skyrocketed to a ridiculous.

(Interestingly, I delivered a commentary on college tuition getting beyond the reach of many students on a television news show in Rochester, New York in 1979. I was invited to appear after the producer read an editorial I wrote on the subject for our school paper.)

But CNN Money reports that the unemployment rate among those with only a high school degree is about double that of people with a college degree.

And those with a college degree earn on average around twice as much money a week as those who did not go to college.[1]

So the statistics would seem not to support Mr. Investment Guru's anti-college stance.

---

[1] http://money.cnn.com/infographic/economy/college-degree-earnings/

He does note that, for the most part, if you want to enter a trade or profession – doctor, lawyer, CPA, engineer, scientists – you need college, both to gain the knowledge and skills, as well as to obtain the credential that will get you hired.

If I did not have a BS in chemical engineering, IBM would not have offered me a $23,000 a year job as a process engineer at their semiconductor plant in Binghamton, NY in 1979.

Mr. Investment Guru notes that you can take courses online or play CDs from The Teaching Company while driving in your car.

I am all for being an autodidact – which means educating yourself through reading and study on your own.

But for many of us, the best education is a combination of self-education with formal schooling.

There were so many difficult concepts I had trouble understanding in my reading of science and engineering, I needed experts (professors) to explain them and answer questions.

When you listen to an audio CD, you can't ask it questions.

Also, while some teenagers are mature, many are not, and I was in the latter category.

So being away at college is a maturing experience I sorely needed.

The other common complain I hear about college is, "Don't go, because it just prepares you to be a corporate tool;

start your own business instead – you'll have more freedom and make more money."

The problem with the "everyone should own their own business" school of thinking is that it assumes having a job is universally terrible and everyone hates it.

But I know many people who prefer being employees. They have no stomach for the marketing and selling which is required of most small business owners. They are quite content being given work to do and then doing it well.

In my case, I was perfectly content in my two corporate jobs. I only moved because in my second job, I was told I had to relocate from Manhattan to Wichita, Kansas, and I did not want to.

Not up to another job search, I asked myself whether there was anything I did in my job as an advertising manager I could offer as a freelance service.

And that's how I got into freelance copywriting.

One more thing....

For my first few years as a freelance copywriter, I specialized almost exclusively in industrial writing.

Prospects challenged me: "How can you understand our products? They are technical?"

I had a five-word answer: "I am a chemical engineer."

And that was all it took to overcome their one major objection – that a copywriter could not understand their products – and get hired.

CHAPTER 39

Five Articles for Your E-Newsletter

I write and distribute to you my subscriber two essays a week. They're free. You can unsubscribe any time. And you can sign up here: www.bly.com/reports

You also get two sales messages a week.

I am often asked, "How do you come up with so much stuff to write about, week after week without fail. Don't you get tired and run out of ideas?"

Now, I am a big advocate of publishing your own e-newsletter, because it is one of the best ways to build a large opt-in e-list ... and to establish a good relationship with your subscribers. Doing so builds trust that leads to sales.

"But where do you get ideas for all those newsletter seemingly without end?" I am asked (I have been publishing this online newsletter since 2004).

If you wish to publish an e-newsletter – whether sporadically, monthly, or weekly – all of which can work ... let me share with you my few simple sources of ideas and inspiration:

#1–Things I learn.

If you are an active practitioner in your field, and given the breakneck speed with which new techniques and developments are invented, you are learning all the time.

Many of my article are based on things I learn doing and observing marketing.

I don't invent most of them. I merely study and then explain them clearly in my newsletter essays.

2–Things I see.

When I observe and admire a particularly clever or effective marketing campaign, I tell you about it here – so you can learn it and perhaps adapt it to your business.

3–Things I know.

After almost 40 years as a copywriter and marketer, I've seen, read, and tested a lot of things most other marketers have not.

Many of them are evergreen, and I present these rules and tactics here for you – hidden gems not 1 in 100 of your competitors even know about – giving you an almost unfair advantage.

4–Rants.

When I see people repeatedly making egregious marketing mistakes, ignoring time-tested principles, or saying things that are wrong or stupid, I report their errors (not naming the person responsible) so you can learn from their mistakes.

I call these "rants" (a term commonly used in info marketing) because I do tend to get worked up about it. I have a highly sensitive B.S. detector and share what it detects with you – often in opinionated and forceful terms.

5–Recommendations.

Whether it is a new book, no course, new guru or expert you should take a closer look at, a new course, or a new resource or vendor, you'll read about it here.

I would go on, but I hope these 5 sources can launch or improve your own e-newsletter.

As for frequency, start with monthly. If open rates are good and unsubscribe rates low, test going to weekly.

If the unsubscribe rate doesn't spike, then your subscribers like your missives well enough to want one a week.

Since at least half of your messages should be content, and half or fewer sales pitches, a weekly newsletter gives you at least one opportunity to sell a product a week.

Which can substantially increase your online revenues to the $100,000 to $200,000 a year level or more – a stream of passive income that can make your life easier without you working too hard to get it.

Who wouldn't want that?

CHAPTER 40

The Trouble with Online Reviews

Anybody who is in the public eye on the Internet ... even someone as minor as me ... will invariably get his fair share of people who feel compelled to bash him – often in a nasty and mean-spirited way.

Of course the conventional wisdom is to shrug it off. But I find it difficult not to take it personally.

For instance, MM writes:

"I have purchased several of Bob's products on his Websites and found them to be a complete rip-off. He charges $50 for 80 pages of useless, outdated content."

It's easy for me to prove that MM is by far a minority opinion; take a look at some of the testimonials from my e-newsletter, book, and e-book readers:

http://www.bly.com/newsite/Pages/Testimonials.html

Also, most of my e-books are in the $29 to $39 range, not $50 (though a couple are).

MM's comment proves to me something I read in an article in a PC magazine decades ago:

"The best thing about the Internet is that anyone can post anything to it.

"The worst thing about the Internet is that anyone can post anything to it.

Evidence of the latter statement is that an article on Quora reporting a Harvard study concluding that one out of five reviews on Yelp are fake.

And on one occasion, a reviewer gave my new book a one-star review saying I hadn't been polite to him when he asked me a question online; he had not even read the book.

Amazon says reviews cannot be personal vendettas and have to be based on a review of the book itself – though I have pointed out that this review is based on a personal incident – and yet Amazon has ignored my 3 requests to have it removed on that basis.

Also, back in the day, book reviewers were written by professional book reviewers who often had a background and knowledge in the topic of the book – and these were vetted by a newspaper or magazine editor prior to publication.

Now online review on Amazon and elsewhere are written by any Tom, Dick, and Harry with a computer and an Internet connection. They are not required to have any working knowledge of the topic of the book and no editor is there to make sure the reviews are civil, literate, and accurate.

Which do you prefer – book reviews by professional reviewers, as in the New York Times Book Review or the New York Review of Books?

Or the opinions of consumers, which range from honest and smart to pure Bozo?

CHAPTER 41

The GIGO Principle in Copywriting

If you are a marketing manager ... copywriter ... ad agency ... creative director ... or content marketer ...

... the marketing you produce is only as good as they information you are able to gain on your target market and your product – and your understanding of them.

Therefore, in the profession of marketing, we ad writers are extremely dependent on our clients.

The better the briefing and research they provide us, the better our copy will be.

Conversely, when we copywriters lack either enough information on the product and the market – or worse, have wrong information – it's extremely unlikely that the promotion will be a home run.

Computer programmers call this GIGO, which stands for "garbage in, garbage out."

So we need good background information – and not garbage – to write the best ad we can.

Yet it is our responsibility as ad creators to help our clients and guide them so they get the right information to us ... and enough of it to write a kick-butt promotion!

Some people call the transfer of product and market knowledge from the client to the marketing creator the "discovery process."

I find it useful to post my own discovery process on my Website and refer clients to it – so they can see the kind of information we need to gather and share to create winners: http://www.bly.com/newsite/Pages/documents/HTPFAC.html

Getting the right information from the client is so important, I outline the responsibilities of both me, the copywriter, and the client, in my standard agreement as follows:

CLIENT AND COPYWRITER RESPONSIBILITIES

As your freelance copywriter, Bob Bly is responsible for:

- Requesting all the information he needs to write your promotion.
- Writing the strongest copy possible.
- Making any revisions you ask for within the terms of the copywriting agreement.
- Always telling you the absolute truth about any of your ideas, edits, or plans – even if it's something you may not want to hear and could even possibly upset you.
- Keeping the client's project confidential.

As the client, you are responsible for:

- Providing Bob with the information about your product, offer, and market he requests for the writing of your copy.

- Being as specific as possible about any edits, revisions, or changes you want Bob to make to his copy draft.

I can't force the client to comply, and of course I always do the best job possible with whatever materials I have to work with.

But by taking on the responsibility of assisting your clients in providing what you need in the discovery process, you greatly increase the odds of having a winning promotion.

Which is good for both you and your client.

I also think guiding the discovery process proactively means you are meeting your fiduciary responsibility to the client by doing due diligence to the best possible level.

GIGO is such an important issue in computer programming and IT that years ago, IBM had an entire course to ensure that the input wasn't garbage.

The course was called "Defining User Requirements for IT Projects," and it was for both the systems creators as well as the system users.

The most common complaint from users about IT is that the project was completed late, over budget, and was not what the users wanted.

IT's most common complaint was that users cannot articulate what they really want, do not understand what resources would be required to create their system, and then complain when you give them what they SAID they wanted.

CHAPTER 42

The Secret of M-Day

For decades, I have been a semi-workaholic who works 11 to 12 hour days and rarely takes a vacation.

But I do have a technique I want to share with you for giving yourself a break once a month.

It makes you feel as if you are playing hooky for the day, though in fact, you are getting a lot done.

I call it "M-Day" or "Miscellaneous Day."

Each month, I pick one day.

It has to be a day when I have no pressing deadlines, no phone meetings, no other appointments, and nothing to deliver to a client or publisher due that same week.

Normally, I schedule my work during the day so I am working on one project or another during every hour, with a short rest between hour increments.

On Miscellaneous Day, there is no schedule. So I don't HAVE to do anything at any particular time.

I crank up the music.

And I spend M-Day working on whatever project or task strikes my fancy.

Then I jump to something else ... well, whenever the mood strikes me.

I often start the day with easy, light work – like a magazine article, working on one of my info marketing projects, or writing an article for my e-newsletter, as I am doing right now.

But often I will get inspired to tackle one or more tougher jobs on M-Day ... such as a particularly challenging sales letter ... and if that mood strikes me, I do it with great gusto.

And somehow, because of the immense freedom I have on M-Day, if anything I enjoy it even more than usual (and I really enjoy writing sales letters) ... and do it even better and faster than usual!

M-Day is also a good day for me to handle miscellaneous tasks that I often put aside because of my usual multiple writing deadlines, such as filling out paperwork or straightening out the occasional problem with a health insurance claim or similar stuff. Miscellany that is boring and distasteful, but still need to be done.

(For instance, recently my health insurance didn't pay a provider because they said my other health insurance carrier should handle it. And you guessed it, I do not HAVE another insurance plan. They are my sole carrier. But I had to spend time on the phone and filling out forms to prove it before they would pay the claim!)

For me, M-Day relaxes and revitalizes me, while giving me a full day in the office that is different and therefore even more fun than usual. And, it is always a very productive day – not really a hooky day at all!

I think it's the change of pace in an otherwise fairly set routine that is part of the secret of M-Day – it's a full-day "pattern interruption."

The other aspect is, with all the projects I can work on during M-Day to choose from, I feel like a kid in a candy store, picking whatever I want as the mood strikes me. There is a big smile on my face and a lightness of spirit that is so invigorating!

So why don't I do more Miscellaneous Days?

One M-Day a month is just about right for me. I tried doing two Miscellaneous Days a few months ago, and it didn't feel right – I felt like a slacker. You may be different.

My suggestion is that you try giving yourself a Miscellaneous Day soon.

If it works for you as it does for me, give yourself one M-Day every month of the year.

You will thank me for it.

Time to sign off now and get back to more M-Day fun!

CHAPTER 43

Should You Write a Business Book?

My FB friend BL writes:

"We need fewer books by people who feel having a book is good for their career. If you're going to write a business book, take time to put some meaty information in it. It pisses me off when I spend good money on a fluffy 'ego' book."

It may surprise you, but I agree with BL.

"Wait a minute, Bob, you hypocrite," you may be thinking. "You have written dozens of books on marketing and copywriting to boost your career. Talk about the pot calling the kettle black!"

Well, here's what you may not see....

Yes, the business books I have written certainly have boosted my freelance writing career and helped build my reputation in the marketing field.

But, that was a byproduct of writing the books – although I was well aware of that benefit and it was a part of the motivation for doing them.

My main reason for writing how-to books has always been this....

Whenever I learn new skills or information of a practical nature, I feel immediately compelled to put what I know into a book about the topic.

Especially when I feel my grasp of the material is strong and my application of it has been effective.

So my primary motivation for how-to book authorship is to teach ... to pass on what I know to others.

This has three benefits:

First, it creates a loyal readership that appreciates the books I write, so that they continue to by new books and other info products by me as they are released.

Second, writing a book builds your reputation as an expert in your field, which in turn helps promote you and your services.

Third – and this is the one most non-authors don't realize – writing a book on a subject probably teaches you as much or more as the people who buy and read your book!

That's because writing a book forces you to do further research on your topic ... think more deeply about it ... organize your material more logically ... and then explain it so clearly that even a newbie can easily understand, enjoy, and profit from it.

By the way, the same is true of teaching a course in the subject.

So IMHO, writing a book or teaching a course on your specialty is one of the most worthwhile activities you can pursue.

On the other hand, some people only write their nonfiction book for the sole purpose of achieving guru status.

This has resulted in a tidal wave of the fluffy "ego" books BL is talking about.

If you ever read a business book and think, "This is a book that should never have been written," you are reading a fluffy ego book produced solely to promote the author, and not to educate the world or even herself.

CHAPTER 44

Research for Copywriting Projects

Subscriber JL writes:

"Hello. I was hoping that you could do a few posts about research.

"How much time do you spend just on product research for a copywriting job?

"Where do you start and how do you know when you are finished?"

Well, as to the first question, I would say that of the total time I spend on a copywriting project, 25% to 40% is spent on research.

By "research" I mean:

–Reading the background material the client provides.

–Reading the additional research I request from my freelance online researcher.

–Doing additional research on my own.

I start by reading everything the client gives me, and then going on to supplement with additional research by me and my researcher.

The research materials I study for a copywriting project generally cover three areas:

–Information about the product.

–Information about the market.

–Copies of promotions for competing products.

As to the second question, I created this short video to give you as precise an answer as to when you know you are finished:

I've already said where I start – with the background materials the client has provided.

And as for when to start, I would say: start within 24 hours of getting the assignment.

Reason: If you put off research, you may find that when the deadline is around the corner, then it's too late. You don't have enough time to do a proper research job and still get A-level copy written on time.

The late, great David Ogilvy said, "Advertising people who ignore research are as dangerous as generals who ignore decodes of enemy signals."

One more thing....

My client AS has said to me repeatedly, "To get a big idea for a winning promotion, you have to do research until you find it in in the research materials."

I would add that sometimes the great promo idea leaps out at you and strikes like a bolt of lightning the instant you come across it.

Other times, it doesn't come easily. You have to dig and dig. But you almost always find something good eventually in the research. And if you are lucky, you often find something great.

CHAPTER 45

The Theory of Haste-Based Rudeness

More and more people today are curt, cold, unfriendly, mean, and downright rude.

But I believe most of them are not bad people, and they aren't in many instances deliberately being mean or rude to you.

They are curt and impolite because they are just so darned busy!

I call this phenomenon haste-based rudeness.

People used to be kinder and more polite.

But especially in business, they are just so swamped, they are always crazy/busy.

And as a result, feel compelled to get through every conversation as rapidly as possible.

This leads to the impression that they are rude for two reasons.

First, everything is fast. They want to get the conversation done as fast as possible. Which may make the other person feel they are getting the brush-off. Also, the tone of a rapid-fire conversation is not genteel.

Second, they are in such a rush, when you try to get a word in, they feel you are interrupted. When you try to express your opinion, they view is as arguing – and they get irritated.

If you are a client, customer, or the boss, you do have power over certain people, and may feel t's OK to treat them dismissively or brusquely.

It's even worse if a boss is talking to an underling, or a vendor to a client, because they are the ones in a position of power.

But as Ben Parker tells his nephew Peter Parker in Spider-Man: "Just because you can do something to someone doesn't mean you should do it."

So what can you do? And how can you act better

A few suggestions....

First, if you find yourself being short or impatient with others, slow down.

If you are stressed, close your door or put on ear buds, and listen to something relaxing and soothing. Beethoven's Moonlight Sonata works for me.

Then do a little deep breathing. Only then do you open the door, invite the person in, and start the meeting or conversation. You will be less rude because you are calmer.

Second, if you find others being rude with you, and they are the boss, client, team leader, or even fellow team member, don't lose your cool.

If you respond with a smile and a non-angry rebuttal, but reply in a softer, measured voice, which will usually get them to back off and match your more reasoned demeanor.

On occasion someone will say something that is incredibly rude, offensive, insulting, or inappropriate.

Pause a second, look the person in the eye, and firmly but calmly say, "What was your purpose in saying that to me?"

8 out of 10 people will instantly realize they were inappropriate, apologize, and continue in a more civil tone. Try it.

For the 2 out of 10 who don't, at least you have made them aware that their words and demeanor crossed a line – and most people do not want to do that.

A warning: Being rude or nasty, even if you didn't mean to be, can come back to bite you.

It can alienate friends, make relationships with relatives frosty, make your spouse and kids to rebel against you, cause colleagues to badmouth you, and demotivate vendors and employees who otherwise normally give you nothing but their best effort.

So even if you are super-busy, force yourself to slow down, smile, and be nice. It will pay big dividends in your business and personal relationships. The people you deal with will be happier with you. And you'll feel better about yourself, too.

CHAPTER 46

Freelancing – Not All Sunshine and Roses

Don't get me wrong.

I would much rather be self-employed than working for a company.

But I do think the idea of being your own boss and starting a home business is a bit oversold by promoters of courses on how to do those things.

Their marketing tells you the many advantages of being a freelance, solopreneur, or small business owner ... and most of what they say is true to one degree or another.

But what they conveniently do not tell you are the drawbacks of being out on your own.

So in the interest of fair play and full disclosure, here are a few of the things that are not so good about being an independent contractor or small business:

1–Every 3 months you have to make a large quarterly payment toward your estimated federal and state (if your state has it) income tax – whether you have cash in the bank or not when the payment due date arrives.

2–If you work at home, you have to empty your own waste basket. I know: that sounds like a small thing. But mine seems filled to overflowing every 15 minutes or so. At Westinghouse, a janitor emptied my trash every night – no cost to me. Now I even have to buy my own trash bags to line the waste can!

3–When you work for someone else, they provide and pay for just about everything. When you are self-employed, you pay for everything from office space and furniture, to computers and photocopiers, to printers and printer ink cartridges (the latter cost a fortune today).

4–There is a health insurance crisis in the U.S. today, and health insurance costs an arm and a leg, no pun intended. But there are few things more dangerous to both your physical and financial health than going without health coverage. A huge problem.

5–Self-employed? No pension for you – and no matching contributions by an employer to your retirement plan. Today fewer and fewer corporate people have these things – but many still do. We freelancers do not. Never had. Never will.

6–Life has gotten more and more expensive today. Incomes to me it seems have not kept pace with inflation. When I got my BS in the late 70s at University of Rochester, it costs me for all 4 years – tuition, room, and board – around $16,000. My son spend 4 years getting his BS at Carnegie Mellon. He graduated 2 years ago, and the total bill was around a quarter of a million dollars – more than 15X what I paid for my degree. I know the average white-collar worker today does not earn 15X what my dad did when I was in school.

7–Freelancers do not have the luxury of getting sick, because we do not get paid sick days. When an employee takes the week off with bronchitis, his corporation chugs along fine without him, as coworkers take up the slack. If I were home sick for a week, not only would my copywriting business make no money, but I would worry and fret about clients, projects, and deadlines.

8—My friend KK has been in IT with his company for over 3 decades and at this point gets 5 full weeks of paid vacation a year. I have never taken more than a week-long vacation, typically one a year, in my life. For many years I only took long weekends, because the demands of my clients did not allow me to be gone for an entire week.

9—Most freelancer writers work alone, sitting in a room, with no co-workers to chat with. While I am usually fine with that, you can, like Jesse the Maytag repairman, get lonely. In a corporate job you spend a lot of time near and with team members and other coworkers.

10—Many small businesses have a crisis-lull-crisis rhythm: they are either too busy and pressured to fill orders on time, or they are slow and in need of more work and cash flow. For them, it either rains or pours – and only rarely is the workload at a happy middle ground.

And believe me, this is far from a comprehensive list of the dark side of being an entrepreneur or independent contractor. I could easily double the number of items.

So to paraphrase Sylvester Stallone's speech to his son in Rocky Balboa – the freelance life ain't all sunshine and roses. Be warned.

But for me and many others I know, it sure beats the alternative.

CHAPTER 47

The 80/20 Formula for Freelance Writing Success

I hear from hundreds of freelance writers each year, many of whom are not entirely happy with their careers.

And they fall into two distinct groups:

>> The first group is freelancers who are primarily pursuing their literary or journalistic calling.

They mostly write plays, poems, movies, novels, nonfiction books, essays, short stories, screenplays, and whatever else they are passionate about.

They love what they do. And find it fulfilling.

Only problem is: most writers in this first group tell me they are hardly making any money ... and are barely getting by.

>> The second group is freelance writers who pursue high-paying commercial projects.

These assignments include technical articles for scientific and medical journals ... white papers ... long-firm direct response sales letters ... video sales letters ... Websites ... speeches ... and many other lucrative gigs.

Most of the writers in this group who reveal their income to me say they are earning $100,000 to $200,000 a year or more.

As a result, they can afford to live in a nice house in a good neighborhood ... pay tuition for their kids at Ivy League colleges ... take great vacations at five-star resorts ... drive late-model luxury cars ... and build a big enough IRA to retire secure for life.

Only problem is: many tell me that, while this commercial writing pays the bills, it doesn't fulfill them artistically.

The solution for both groups is simple. I call it "the 80/20 formula for freelance writing success."

The formula says you spend 80% or so of your time on high-paying projects for commercial clients – and the other 20% on your literary, journalistic, and artistic writings.

By spending 80% of your time on high-profit writing, you earn enough money to provide well for your family – while remaining freelance and avoiding having to work at a 9-to-5 job for someone else.

But by spending the other 20% of your time writing for fun and artistic fulfillment, you also get to write the things that matter most to you.

And because of your cash flow from the high-paying 80% of your work, you don't even need to make a dime from your more literary endeavors – although for some of us it does in fact generate additional, and in some cases even significant, cash flow.

By the way, the magic of the formula is that you spend some time writing what others will pay you a lot of money to write ... and some time writing things for your own pleasure, self-expression, and amusement – whether they pay well, poorly, or not at all.

There is no magic, however, about the actual ratio. You can adjust it to fit your temperament and needs. For instance, I do 90/10, not 80/20, and that works for me.

Full disclosure: the great advantage I have is that I actually love writing the high-profit stuff – in my case, copy.

Some writers do. Others not so much. But the 80/20 formula works in either case. Try it!

Ted Nicholas and others have written that you need 4 elements to have a happy and successful life – meaningful work you enjoy, money, close personal relationships, and good health.

By following the 80/20 formula, you will have the first two items on Ted's list in abundance: meaningful work you enjoy as well as money.

For the next two – meaningful relationships and good health – you are on your own for.

CHAPTER 48

You Won an Award. Now What?

Recently I got a press release from ad agency Imbue Creative.

The headline: "Imbue Creative Wins Three Communicator Awards from the Academy of Interactive Visual Arts in Logo, Packaging, and Non-Profit Brochure Categories."

You can imagine how interested I was in this important, timely, and useful news.

(Yes, that's meant sarcastically.)

It's typical when you win an award to send out a press release about it. And I am not saying you shouldn't.

After all, some of your industry and local media outlets may pick it up and give you a quick mention, which certainly doesn't hurt.

And you may indeed get inquiries or even business as a result of the award announcement.

However, the number of award-winning ad campaigns that absolutely failed to produce positive results is legend.

For instance, the communications director of the now-defunct Outpost.com bragged out one of their TV spots that it won all kinds of awards including several Clio's – and the advertising, marketing, and creative communities love it.

But she followed up by admitting, "It generated no increase in sales. And it pissed of the shareholders."

Advertising Age magazine wrote that while the commercial on those Clio's, the problem was that it did not make clear to consumers what Outpost actually sold online, which was computer products.

Despite the cache awards may give ad agencies and even their clients within the industry, consumers often view these honors with great indifference.

In your PR, your time and energy is better spent creating and disseminating content of real value – from tips and surveys, to how-to e-book and white papers – than this type of "brag and boast" PR.

A more grievous offense, at least to me as a direct response marketer, is the quote that appears later in the release from Imbue VP Michael Piperno.

He says, ""We are delighted to be recognized for creative excellence by The Communicators Awards in the different categories."

Marketers who know what they are doing value response and measured results – including leads, sales, and profits – over "creative excellence" all day long.

"Creative" agencies make a living out of preying on foolish businesspeople who value creativity over sales, just as these agencies do, too.

CHAPTER 49

Dodging a Bullet

It's been observed many times that you need 4 things to enjoy a happy and successful life:

>> Meaningful work.

>> Money.

>> Personal relationships.

>> Good health.

Well, I have several of these thing, a lot of the time.

Recently, I dodged a major bullet – in the health department.

Here's what happened....

After a routine physical, I got a call from Linda in my doctor's office.

"Dr. RS says your blood protein levels are a bit high, and he wants you to see a hematologist."

I went to the hematologist's Website ... and discovered the words "hematology and oncology" in the name of the practice.

Not exactly encouraging.

So I saw the hematologist, Dr. FB, who said the high blood protein could mean I have blood cancer – multiple myeloma.

To find out, he ordered a battery of additional blood protein tests ... and had me go for a full-body x-ray of every bone in my body.

Apparently, if you have myeloma, it can weaken and fracture your bones.

The results came back. Not negative. Not positive. But inconclusive.

"At this point, I think your risk of having cancer is lower than I originally believed – I would say down to 20%," he said.

"But you could still have bone cancer."

So he did a bone marrow biopsy with a needle through the bone near the bottom of my spine where it connects to the pelvic bone.

It took a week to get the results.

I was not particularly on edge, but my mother and wife were becoming frantic (I did not tell my kids).

Finally, a week later, Dr. FB called and immediately said: "Bob, this is Dr. FB, and you do not have bone cancer" – in a cheery voice, no preamble, exactly as such news should be delivered.

So for now, I am free and clear.

But it's a reminder.

Remember that list of the 4 things you need to be happy?

I believe they are nearly equal.

But health is perhaps a little more equal than the others.

KS, a friend who is a cancer survivor, commented when he read the line above: "I come to believe exactly the same thing. It's the bedrock on which pretty much everything else in life is dependent."

When you or your loved ones have health worries or problems, it's one of the most difficult things in life to cope with.

And brings to mind the old saying:

"Every day you wake up above the ground is a good day."

One odd note to the story....

When Dr. FB was doing the spinal tap, I heard him say softly, "Uh-oh."

Again, not something you want to hear.

I asked him what was wrong.

He said, "The needle bent on your bone and did not penetrate."

I asked if that was unusual.

He said it had never happened before.

And that based on this, and my bone x-ray, I have extraordinarily dense bones.

I asked if that was bad or caused by disease.

He said no. It was a good thing.

As people get old, many have weakening bone, making them more susceptible to fracture or osteoporosis.

And with my super-dense bones, Dr. FB explained, while I might have future health worries, brittle bones would never be one of them.

He tried again, and was successful, after great effort, on the second biopsy attempt.

CHAPTER 50

Nostalgia for the Good Old Days

Yes, today the world is filled with modern marvels that make life better, easier, safer, healthier, and more profitable.

Examples include personal computers, smart phone, the Internet, e-mail, self-driving cars, drones, and new medical treatments for everything from arthritis to cancer.

But, as much as I like and embrace many innovations, I do sometimes long for the good old days.

In particular, here are a few of the things I miss from way back when, illogical as some items on the list may seem:

1—My IBM Selectric typewriter.

Ever since getting my first PC in 1982, computers have helped my freelance writing income skyrocket.

That being said, I loved the feel of the Selectric keyboard … the freedom from worrying about malware and other computer glitches … and the experience of seeing my words immediately appear on paper as I typed them.

2—Vinyl records.

Vinyl records are making a comeback. The main advantage of records is that the large album covers had plenty of room for extensive liner notes.

CDs have these notes printed on separate insert booklets, which quickly become lost. And somehow they are not as fun to read.

My kids love iPods and digital music. But I don't want to own yet another device, and I have no need to carry 950 songs with me.

3—Newspapers.

When I was young my ambition was to be a newspaper reporter, which was considered one of the coolest jobs for writers on the planet. After all, Superman was a reporter!

The millennials seem not to read the newspaper anymore. And today, a newspaper report is ranked as one of the least desirable jobs.

4—Easy air travel.

I have never liked travel of any kind.

But air travel in the 70s was an order of magnitude better than it is today – for three reasons.

First, planes were often half-empty. Now, they are almost always full. An ancillary benefit was that there was always room to store your luggage in the overhead.

Second, there was more legroom. Today, there is so little, it even bothers me … and I'm a short guy.

Third, pre-911, security was so much laxer, because it didn't seem to need to be otherwise.

You didn't have to take off your shoes, jacket, and belt, which to me is a pain in the rear.

5—The ability to unplug.

In some ways, smart phones and other mobile devices are a blessing.

For instance, I worry about my kids less, because I can always reach them on their cell phones.

On the other hand, wireless connectivity has created a society in which we are continually connected and available to our boss, coworkers, and customers round the clock. Putting us under even more stress.

6—Chocolate milk shakes.

The greater awareness of nutrition today keeps us healthier and may even extend our lives, and that's a great thing.

On the other hand, in the 60s we mostly ate stuff that tasted good, either blissfully unaware or not caring whether it was good for us.

In particular, I miss regularly consuming chocolate milk shakes ... barbecue ribs ... salami sandwiches ... Coke ... and even the occasional Ring Ding.

6—Safe sex.

I got married before AIDS reared its ugly head, so I dodged a bullet – not that I was promiscuous anyway.

But back then, at least casual hookups and active dating were not potentially life-ending activities.

I can't imagine that single people who are sexually active today with multiple partners aren't constantly worried about getting HIV.

7—The Beatles, Sinatra, and Elvis.

Call me old-fashioned, but I don't understand how people enjoy songs when you cannot understand the lyrics being sung or rapped.

Some people say Will Smith is a terrible rapper. But he is one of the clearest, most articulate rapper out there (Eminem is, too).

8–Classic cars.

I liked the way cars looked and drove back in the day better than today's modern tin cans.

My dream car is a fully restored 1957 Pontiac Chieftain.

My mother bought one used in the 60s for $100.

It still pains me enormously that my parents sold it to a guy who totaled the car soon after he bought it.

What a putz he was to destroy that treasure!

CHAPTER 51

A Lesson in Education from Good Will Hunting

Ben Settle sent out an e-mail last month that precisely expressed, more articulately than I have...

...my own sentiments about what's wrong with selling outrageously expensive coaching and training programs online to newbies:

"I'm not a big fan of high ticket coaching and masterminds that are targeted to people who are newbies, desperate, or don't have the money, experience, or the knowledge to put the info into context.

"Even with my own products, I tell people not to buy if they have to go into debt over it. They should get their financial houses in order first."

I applaud Ben's ethical and sensible stance here. He explains that his objection mirrors his own experience as an info products buyer when he was a newbie:

"I simply didn't have the money to afford all the high priced stuff. I started with low priced books like Dan Kennedy's Ultimate Sales Letter, for example, which was like $8.

"Then, when I was able to afford it (using money earned from applying what I learned in the first book), started spending money on the more expensive stuff."

HK, one of my friends and colleagues, pointed out that some people have spent their last dime to attend training on a money-making venture they really wanted to pursue, learned it, applied the learning, and became spectacularly successful at it.

I know this is true, as several of my readers and students have achieved precisely this kind of success.

The problem is, they are outliers. As for the rest, most of the people who spend $5,000 for a training never recover a fraction of the investment, if any.

If you are interested in a topic and a guru, here's the order in which you should acquire his or her knowledge:

>> First, read and get all the free stuff only – their e-newsletter, free ebooks, free special reports, online articles, blog, free Webinars.

>> Second, most gurus have one or more conventional paperbound books, usually selling for around $15 new, a few bucks on Amazon, or available free at your local library. These books have much the same content as their $200 multimedia home study course or even their $1,000 coaching.

>> Third, when and only when you have exhausted the free and low-cost supply of the guru's content, then move up to one of his more costly paid products – but just one to start. And always make sure there is an unconditional money-back guarantee with a 30 to 90-day return window.

Do not fool yourself, like many students at Ivy League universities do, that a higher price automatically means better content, better learning, and better results.

It's like Matt Damon's character explains in Good Will Hunting to an obnoxious Harvard grad student: "You're spending $50,000 for an education you could have gotten for a dollar-fifty in late fees at the public library."

CHAPTER 52

Three Steps to Stamping Out Boring Copy

"There are a lot of sins in life," Senator Lindsey Graham was quoted as saying in New York magazine. "But the one that's intolerable is being bored. I hate boring."

The problem with saying that something is "boring," however, is that the statement is meaningless unless you ask: "Boring to WHOM?"

For instance, I recently had the assignment of writing, for a major chemical company, a white paper on "clean agent fire suppression systems for data centers."

While this topic would put the majority of copywriters I know into a coma, for me, being a chemical engineer and former chemistry major, it was absolutely fascinating – and pure joy.

Especially in sales copy, being boring is an absolute sin and a sure road to lack of interest and dismal response rates.

As David Ogilvy once observed, "You cannot sell the consumer by boring her to death.

So ... how do you avoid being bored with your copywriting projects as well as boring prospects with the copy you write?

Making sure the copy you write is not boring is a three-step process:

>> Step one is to, as much as is humanly possible, only take on assignments that – if they don't absolutely fascinate you – at least are interesting to you.

That way, you don't have to fake enthusiasm, because you will enjoy learning about that idea and selling it to others.

>> Step two is to dig into the topic to find the area of it with the greatest interest to the reader.

One high-tech copywriter told me, "The most fascinating thing about technology is that people invented it."

Joseph Kelly, a former speechwriter for Eisenhower, said: "There is a kernel of interest in everything man or God made."

Your job is to find that kernel, though in copy, it must either arouse curiosity, stimulate readership, or make the sale.

>> Step three is to do the hard work of research.

Most copywriters I know enjoy learning, so the research is fun reading and intellectually stimulating.

Second, specifics make copy both more interesting and more believable.

Generalities bore the reader and cause her to quickly lose interest and click away.

There are two bonus steps to making sure you are never bored as a c copywriter:

>> Step four: Always have multiple writing projects.

Isaac Asimov said the secret to his great writing productivity was having many projects, so when he got bored or tired or just felt he could go further with his book that day...

...he switched to his columns and articles on a different topic, which kept gave him a fresh subject.

>> Step five: Write things other than copy.

My 80/20 rule for copywriters is to spend 80% of your time writing copy for clients.

This is the key to a six-figure annual income year after year.

But to vary things up, spend 20% of your time with non-copy writing projects that are purely yours.

Mark Ford writes poetry, short stories, and movie scripts.

I write short stories and had a book of them come out from Quill Drive Books in 2016.

I have also had a blast on writing nonfiction books on everything from sex and Star Trek, to careers and satire.

Plus, I did cartoons and wrote the occasional newspaper or magazine article, published in periodicals ranging from Cosmopolitan and Writer's Digest, to New Jersey Monthly and the and City Paper.

This keeps me fresh and ensure I am virtually never bored, except by paperwork, which I loathe.

CHAPTER 53

Beware the Boob Tube

We were invited to a backyard barbecue a few weeks ago by our friend AE and her husband JE.

Whenever we get together, JE starts recommending to me TV shows he has become hooked on and finds interesting – and think I will also like.

I always explain politely, every time we are together, that thanks but no thanks – I have no interest and will never take a look at any of these shows.

One reason is the increasing popularity of shows that are episodic, such as Lost was, requiring you to watch every week – or save them up and binge-watch multiple episodes in one sitting.

I avoid the shows he recommends because (a) I fear I might indeed get hooked and (b) watching TV shows are a time-suck that more often than not (c) rots your brain.

Neuroscientists who took MRI scans of 290 children ages 5 to 18 found that anatomical changes inside the youngster's brains after prolonged TV viewing actually lowered IQ.[2]

In effect, watching too much TV has now scientifically been proven to make people stupider.

---

[2] http://blog.brainfacts.org/2015/05/watching-tv-alters-childrens-brain-structure-and-lowers-iq/#.WCC8ki0rKUk

"Well, if you don't watch TV then what do you do?" JE asks me, genuinely puzzled.

I explain that the two activities I substitute for TV are reading and writing.

Writing is mainly my vocation. Though I love it so much, I can hardly call it "work."

Reading is my favorite spare time activity.

I read widely, both fiction and nonfiction books of all types.

But this too is part of work, in that reading (a) provides grist for the copywriting mill, enabling me to acquire all sorts of knowledge that invariably finds its way into my promotions.

And (b) reading and writing are the two best ways to become a better writer – so reading is in essence my ongoing continuing education as a writer.

Avoiding lots of TV allows me to spend more time writing and reading, two activities that are much more active and beneficial than TV, which is passive and mind-numbing.

I do sometimes turn on the TV when I am tired and just want to veg out, but I rarely watch more than an hour a day.

What do I watch? We have cable, so I flip until I find a movie that looks interesting and watch part of it, and rarely find it just as it is beginning.

I have to confess that there are certain movies that I will watch repeatedly when I stumble across them on TV; I do not buy movies on DVD.

They include The Book of Eli, Galaxy Quest, Water World, The Postman, Robocop, Dracula Untold, and any movie with Wolverine in it.

If you think my taste is abysmal, then watch what you like and don't worry about what I like.

My favorite TV show of all time is Jacob Bronowski's The Ascent of Man, and I also loved all his books – for me, it's better than Carl Sagan's Cosmos.

CHAPTER 54

Transparency Wins in E-mail Marketing

A few weeks ago, I sent out an e-mail to my list with this subject line:

"My doctor said: 'Bob, you might have blood cancer.'"

My blood test results prompted my family doctor send me to a hematologist because they indicated I might have blood cancer.

Turned out, I dodged a health bullet: no blood cancer.

When I told this story in my e-newsletter, I got well over a hundred of you e-mailing me back – more response than any of my other e-mails in recent memory.

This taught me two things – the first of which warms my heart, and the second of which reveals an important truth about e-mail marketing that may be useful to you.

FIRST, my subscribers, as a group, are kind and caring – really nice people – which is the kind of readers I want to have.

SECOND, that the technique of "transparency" ... revealing a lot of personal information about yourself unrelated to content or selling in your writing ... helps create a bond between you and your subscribers.

Some comments from the responses to my cancer-scare e-mail:

JK: "Thank you for sharing this personal story."

CB: "Thank you for your e-mail communications, which are a pleasure to read and always worth the time. I read every single one."

TP: "Thank you for sharing your personal story and this great lesson for all of us."

AB: "I always enjoy your messages. But special thanks for sharing something so personal. Your humanity is what makes your e-mails stand out from all the others in my inbox."

DF: "Bob, I love your down to earth good old fashioned work ethic and I love your newsletter."

I share these comments not to brag, but to demonstrate my thesis: transparency works in cementing your relationship with your readers.

Result: they trust you more, like you more, and read you more.

And people buy from people they like and trust.

So transparency makes your subscribers enjoy your newsletter, decreasing your unsubscribe rate and boosting your open rates.

And all this translates into greater loyalty and more sales for the products you offer your readers in your e-mails.

CHAPTER 55

On Color and Typography

Subscriber JA writes:

"Bob, have you noticed how many Websites use gray typeface on a white background?

"It's difficult to read.

"How about taking a minute to address the importance of color schemes?"

Entire books have been written about color in design. And I am no expert.

But the whole of it can be boiled down to one principle:

The primary purpose of design is to attract the eye to the copy, and make the text easy to read – and the latter is more important than the former.

Anything that makes the copy difficult to read, no matter how dazzling or graphically innovative, is bad graphic design, whether in print or online.

So at a glance, the color and type rules to follow are these:

1–Make all type large enough to read easily by an older adult with average to less-than-average eyesight.

2–The best color scheme is black type on a white background.

3–In body copy, avoid reverse type, which is white type on a black background.

4—Avoid low-contrast color schemes such as gray type on a white background, or dark blue type on a light blue background, or the horrific but not uncommon gray type on a black background.

5—In print materials, use serif typefaces – letters with little extension on them, such as Times Roman.

6—Online, use sans serif typefaces – letters with no extensions, such as Arial.

7—In direct mail, despite what the vendors of handwritten envelopes and letter mailing say, I have seen no proof that handwritten outer envelopes or handwritten letters outpull typeset. If handwriting universally outperformed typewritten, everyone would use it all the time.

CHAPTER 56

The Joy of Passive Income

One Friday night last month, after checking, answering, and then deleting or filing in Outlook all my e-mail, we left the house at 6pm to get a quick dinner.

When we returned at 7:30pm, I checked my e-mail again.

In the 90 minutes we were out, I had gotten $907 in info product orders online, all for products I was not actively promoting that week.

No work on my part. $900 made while eating in a Korean restaurant.

(Full disclosure: this is an isolated incident and not a typical result.)

Some people work all week to make $900 in a 9-to-5 job that bores them.

One that they must commute to and from on their own time and dime – for a boss they don't like

I tell you this not to brag, but to illustrate (a) the value of having multiple streams of income and (b) the advantage of having at least one of these be a stream of passive income.

Just to be clear, passive income is anything that makes money without your direct labor.

Passive income streams generate positive cash flow for you on Sundays, holidays, vacations, and even while you sleep.

As George Clason writes in his book The Richest Man in Babylon, "I wish an income that will keep flowing into my purse whether I sit upon the wall or travel to far lands."

On the other hand, with active income streams, you get paid only when you are working.

Dentistry, for instance, although lucrative, is strictly an active income stream.

Dentists have a saying: "Unless you are drilling and filling, you are not billing."

Most people I know have, for the most part, only a single stream of income – typically the paycheck from their full-time job, where they toil away to make someone else rich.

And unless you are getting a huge salary, that's risky ... although back in the day, a corporate job gave one the illusion of security.

But no longer.

The scary part is that if you get laid off or the company goes belly up, you suddenly have zero income ... except for a small sum from temporary unemployment insurance.

Your income stops. But your expenses relentlessly keep on coming.

This sudden stoppage of your cash flow makes it extremely difficult to pay your rent, mortgage, car loans, insurance premiums, property tax, and kids' college tuition – among many other expenses.

When I became a full-time freelance writer in February 1982, my main source of money was an active income stream – writing copy for clients.

But even back then, I had a smaller passive income stream: royalties from my hardcover and paperback books published by mainstream publishing houses.

The nice thing about royalties is that your work can generate ongoing income for you months, even years, after you write it.

For instance, I recently got a check from one of my publishers for $4,856 ... for the Chinese edition of a book I wrote in 1985, which is work I completed more than 3 decades ago.

Some of the passive income streams that various writers I know have in place include:

–Book royalties.

–Copywriting royalties.

–Reselling your published articles to multiple magazines and Websites over and over.

–Real estate investing.

–Stocks and bonds.

–Online information marketing.

–Options trading.

Action step: develop at least one active income stream and one passive income stream.

Your goal: Build them to annual six-figure revenues each.

That way, if you decide to quite working someday, you can live comfortably from the passive income stream alone.

CHAPTER 57

The Rise of the Non-Book

I call it "the rise of the non-book."

I'm talking about the increasing number of extremely short Kindle e-books being published and sold on Amazon.

My FB friend TJ describes Kindle as a place "where anyone can string 10,000 words together, make a cover, call it a book, and present it to the world."

Back in the day, when I wrote my first book in 1981, you had to write an actual book to become a "real" author.

For a 200-page trade paperback or hardcover book, that meant writing, on average, about 80,000 words.

Not a monumental task, but quite a bit of work.

Among my 93 published books (plus two more under contract and being written by me even as you read this e-mail), most are around 200 pages.

Yes, a few are only around 100 pages. And I have written half a dozen published children's books that are even shorter.

However, they balance out with several adult nonfiction titles over 300 pages ... and one that is a whopping 800 pages – "The Advertising Manager's Handbook," published by Prentice-Hall.

But today, as TJ points out, you can write a short document – just 10,000 words, 5,000 words, or even less

– slap a nice cover on it, create a Kindle e-book, and sell it online.

When people see it on Amazon, most don't realize it is a glorified report or article – and they mistake it for the author having written a real full-length book.

To self-promoters who want to inflate their guru status, publishing a series of short pieces as individual Kindle e-books is a quick and easy way to make yourself look like a more prolific book author than you really are.

But for actual book authors, like me, it devalues your work and production – because to the untrained eye, it looks like everyone and his brother has written as many books as you have.

This is why I am a fan of paperbound books over Kindle e-books, and of books sold by mainstream publishing houses vs. self-published.

Having a paperbound book with a major publisher doesn't guarantee quality.

But at least the book has been vetted at several levels beyond the author himself – including the literary agent, publishing house editorial committee (they make the decision whether to buy and publish your book), book editor, copy editor, and proofreader.

I know many of you today are self-publishing and Kindle fanatics.

But to borrow phrasing from "Make Mine Marvel" Stan Lee – make mine McGraw-Hill (or Macmillan, or Morrow ... you get the idea.

Having said all this, do I think there is anything wrong with going the non-book route on Kindle?

No.

Would I do it myself if I were just starting out today – and could not sell a full-length book to a traditional publishing house?

You betcha.

CHAPTER 58

The Trouble with Spec Work

Subscriber DC writes:

"In my many years as a freelance copywriter, occasionally a potential client has asked me to write a free 'test piece.' "I've always refused but today the marketing director of a huge European logistics company contacted me with this request:

"'I am evaluating external support for various projects. One such project is for small to medium-size enterprises (SMEs) and logistics.

"'Can you give me some draft ideas of content (blogs, white papers, etc.) that would appeal to SMEs who are looking to broaden their horizons and get more involved in international trade?'"

"So he wants free editorial consultancy work with no guarantee of a contract or payment, and of course he could just take my best ideas!

"This is a variation of the infamous free test piece and it shows how careful we must be about speculative projects.

"I'm sending you this story partly to help other freelancers and I hope it's useful in your excellent newsletter."

I agree with DC: Avoid working "on spec" – on spec meaning you do it with no promise of getting paid.

Spec work means you write the copy for the client for free.

If they like it and decide to use it, they pay you something.

If they don't like it, the project is over – and you don't get a dime for your time and effort.

The idea of working on spec to me is patently ridiculous and grossly offensive.

Try going to your local gas station and telling the attendant: "Fill my car with gas, and if it runs well, I will pay you for it ... but if not, I owe you nothing."

Order a meal at a local restaurant and say to the waiter: "Bring my steak and baked potato; if I like it, I'll pay the bill; if not, I won't."

So if someone asks you, "Write my ad for free, and I will pay for it only if I like and use it. If not, I won't" – well, what writer in his right mind would agree to that?

Samuel Johnson said, "No man but a blockhead ever wrote for any reason other than money."

So if you write on spec for a potential copywriting client, you are the blockhead.

And when you don't get paid, you have no one to blame but yourself.

After all, you asked for it to happen.

Are there ever any exceptions to the no-spec-work rule?

Answer: Precious few.

CHAPTER 59

The Worst Way to Approach a Potential Client

Subscriber HG writes:

"As a big fan of your work, I must confess your Web pages are boring, and I guess they are not converting to sales as they did before, isn't it?

"Please allow me to restore a few of your Web pages from the archaeological ruins to the modern slick, easy to read, search engine friendly, better converting pages, OK?

"If you do not want to make more money, then just neglect this e-mail."

This approach to establishing a relationship with me is really stupid, for 3 reasons....

First, HG does not know my landing page conversion rates. He assumes they are poor.

But as Felix Unger pointed out in an old episode of The Odd Couple, "When you ASSUME you make an ASS of U and ME."

In fact, the pages he cited as failures pull like gangbusters.

They make me so much passive income that, if I so desired, I could quit my freelance copywriting job tomorrow, and never work another day in my life. (But of course that idea is anathema to me.)

Second, even if I was jonesing to improve some of my pages, why would I hire HG? He gives not one shred of proof that he has any skills or success in this area.

Third, the part of his message I left out was even more off-putting and even insulting to me – and insulting strangers rarely wins them over.

When I posted HG's comments on Facebook, one of my FB friends, JS, wrote:

"All he is trying to do is use the same tactics as e-mail spammers that supposedly work on the weak-minded masses.

"He has no persuasive tactics. The entire thing is a pitch. It comes from someone who thinks he is good at manipulation, though in actuality, he sticks out like a sore thumb."

And another FB friend on that same thread, MS, said:

There are a few turn-offs for me with this sort of thing—implying expertise without having researched his assertions, the sense of a little dishonesty through flattery, and a scare tactic infused with some arrogance.

"My reaction, from an open minded perspective and willingness to accept help, is to tell him to take a hike!"

And that's just what I did.

Thanks, MS!

CHAPTER 60

On Not Knowing Stuff

Is there a basic degree of knowledge one should possess as an (a) educated, literature human being and (b) to function competently in one's chosen field?

Though it's difficult to pinpoint exactly what that level of knowledge is, I do think that, yes, there is a body of knowledge that people must possess to be taken seriously in society in general as well as in their industry or profession in particular.

And sadly, I see fewer and fewer people at this level of basic cultural and technical knowledge as the years pass.

For instance, a couple of years ago, Alan Alda was the commencement speak at my son's graduation ceremony at Carnegie-Mellon.

When I told my personal trainer OL, who is in his 30s, he said: "Who?"

Alan Alda – played Hawkeye Pierce on TV in M*A*S*H, I said.

Nope, replied OL. Never heard of him.

Until that moment, it never occurred me that there could be people in this country who aren't familiar with M*A*S*H.

Writer Harlan Ellison tells how, years ago, when he mentioned Dachau at a college lecture, a student raised her hand and asked, "What's Dachau?"

He was flabbergasted that an educated American would not know his infamous concentration camp.

Similarly, I find that in marketing, practitioners lack basic knowledge that I, at least, think they should have.

Early in my career, in the 1980s, when I referred in my copywriting classes to Claude Hopkins and his classic book Scientific Advertising, most students nodded their heads in recognition.

Today, if I am giving a copywriting lecture to an audience of several hundred copywriters and marketers, and I ask "Who here has read Claude Hopkins' Scientific Advertising?" only one or two hands in the room go up – if that – which I find almost beyond belief.

Don't get me wrong: The majority of people I associate with both in my personal and business life are smart, educated, cultured, literate, and knowledgeable.

A huge number of them are a lot smarter than I am ... and know a lot more than I do.

On the other hand, the people who fill the Jerry Springer show studio as his live audience have to come from somewhere, right?

In his book *The Closing of the American Mind* (Simon & Schuster), Allan Bloom wrote:

"The failure to read good books both enfeebles the vision and strengthens our most fatal tendency – the belief that the here and now is all there is."

Do I agree with that? Well, being a big reader, I have to say yes. Or at least note here that I have a difficult time making conversation with people who don't read books.

CHAPTER 61

Portrait of the Writer as an Artist Starving in a Garret

In 2017, as I turn 60, I look back and recall how different young writers were in the 70s when I started submitted my stories to magazines for publication – as compared with the new money-focused young wordsmiths today.

Back then, there was some odd notion that many writers had about it being somehow romantic, cool, and even hip to be struggling in poverty and obscurity ...

... eating Kraft mac and cheese for dinner every night – and the proverbial writer "starving in a garret."

The garret for me being my crappy walk-up tenement studio apartment on Manhattan's Upper East Side.

The goals were art, publication, literature, fame, and the best-seller list first ... and after that, then yes, money.

But for today's writers, who aspire to getting rich in mere weeks by selling information online rather than a novel to HarperCollins (a publisher to which I sold two books on Star Trek), money is the main thing, front and center.

As is evidence by the astounding popularity of all the high-priced "make a million dollars with information marketing online" programs being sold today.

In my day, you learned your craft in copywriting by reading used copies of Ogilvy and Caples books you bought used for a dollar at the Strand.

Now people of all ages, from all walks of life, hand over their credit card to buy training in information marketing and copywriting for thousands of dollars a pop ... without batting an eyelash.

But even in my day, the brighter writers were too smart to buy into the "starving artist" mentality that others embraced.

In his book Factotum, Charles Bukowski, who was poor for a lot of his life, wrote:

"Starvation, unfortunately didn't improve art ... the myth of the starving artist was a hoax.

"A man's art was rooted in his stomach. A man could write much better after eating a porterhouse steak than he could after eating a nickel candy bar."

How true!

And, like J. Jonah Jameson in the first Spiderman movie – who tells Peter Parker, "Freelance is the ticket" –

–Bukowski, like so many other writers, was an advocate of freelancing ... and abhorred 9 to 5 jobs (which he was forced to take for decades until he finally started making good money as a freelance novelist and poet).

Bukoswki in Factotum again:

"How in hell could a man enjoy being awakened at 6:30am by an alarm clock, leap out of bed, dress, force-feed, piss, brush teeth and hair, and fight traffic to get to a place where essentially you made lots of money for somebody else and were asked to be grateful for the opportunity to do so?"

I get this: when I had a 9 to 5 corporate job, I hated setting and waking up to an alarm, perform morning ablutions, put on a suit and tie, and commute to be at work by 8 or 9am.

Ironically, as a freelance, I have gotten up every morning at 6am – without an alarm clock – for decades.

Within 3 minutes of getting up each morning, I walk a flight of steps to my desk, turn on the PC, and start writing immediately.

No need to waste valuable time making sure I am clean shaven, my shirt freshly cleaned and pressed, my shoes shined, my pie hold rinsed with mouthwash, and my hair neatly combed – as I did in my days as an employee in corporate America.

I arise naturally, bright and bushy tailed, eager to dive into the day, because I love freelance writing.

Always have. And hope, think, and am pretty confident I always will.

We'll see.

But now in my 38th year of being a writer – so far, so good.

CHAPTER 62

Client Contact with Strategic Clipping

Though I don't think I invented it, I'm one of an extremely small group of people who use this little-known marketing channel to stay in touch with clients and prospects.

I call it "strategic clipping."

How it works is simple....

Whenever you come across an article in a magazine or newspaper that is relevant to one of your client's business – or even his or her hobbies or personal life – tear or cut it out of the publication ... and mail it to the client.

It sounds trivial. Almost ridiculous for me to call it a marketing channel.

But in fact, it's one of the most effective relationship-building tools ever devised.

First, here's how I do it.

I don't deliberately research material to clip and send to clients.

But in the course of your reading, you will come across many such items weekly.

A lot of people look at a relevant article and think, "Bill would be interested in this; maybe I should send it to him."

But because they are busy, they don't.

I do. It's easy, because my strategic clipping method is fast and efficient ... and takes almost none of my time.

When I see an article for Bill, I tear it out of the publication.

I handwrite in pen a quick note at the top: "Bill – FYI – Bob Bly." That's it. Scribbled in seconds.

I then hand it to my assistant and say, "Please mail this to Bill Jones at Acme Solar Energy."

And that's it. My assistant does the work.

No need for me to take time out of my hectic day to find Bill's postal address, hunt for a stamp and envelope, put the article in the envelope, affix the stamp, seal the envelope, and drive to the post office to drop it in the mail.

If I didn't have an assistant and had to do it myself, I probably would not use strategic clipping. But fortunately, I do have. (Every solopreneurs should.)

Why is strategic clipping so effective? For 3 reasons:

First, the content is extremely targeted and relevant to the recipient.

Second, it has a personal touch – especially the handwritten note.

Third, in our digital age where people are bombarded by e-mail, getting a piece of paper in the mail stands out.

The only drawback to strategic clipping is: it's hit and miss. If I don't come across an article of interested to Bill, he doesn't get a clip.

My solution is to publish a regular e-newsletter.

An e-newsletter is not as customized and personal as a strategic clip.

But the regularity of sending a monthly or weekly newsletter helps build top of mind awareness ... and ensures that my prospects, clients, and customers hear from you on a continual basis.

Also, strategic clipping works online too:

When I get an e-newsletter in my inbox containing a relevant article, I immediately forward it to the appropriate person, also with a brief message – "Bill – FYI ... thought this might interest you – Bob Bly."

Easy as pie.

CHAPTER 63

Add Value to Your Talks with Handouts

When speaking to a group, must you have a leave-behind handout? For a keynote to a large audience at a conference or meeting, a handout could be considered optional, although I would opt for having one.

In virtually every other speaking situation, a handout is highly recommended if not absolutely mandatory. At some conferences, the sponsor actually requires speakers to use PowerPoint and supply their slides as an electronic file audience members can download from the conference Website.

The leave-behind can take one of several formats. It can be hard copy of the PowerPoint slides, brochures, article reprints, or reprints of the typed text of a speech.

The handout can contain the full text of your talk, an outline, just the visuals, or a report or article on a subject that is either related to the presentation topic or expands on one of the subtopics you touched on briefly in the talk. If you use PowerPoint, you can just print out your PowerPoint presentation and use that as the handout.

Every handout should contain your company name, address, phone, e-mail address, and Website URL, and if possible a full resource box with a brief summary of who you are and what you do, as should every marketing document you produce.

If the handout is the full text of your talk or a set of fairly comprehensive notes, tell the audience before starting, "There's no need to take notes. We have hard copies of this presentation for you to take home." This relieves listeners of the burden of note taking, freeing them to concentrate on your talk.

Handouts such as transcripts of a speech, articles, reports, or other materials with lots of copy should be handed out after the talk, not before. If you hand them out before you step up to the podium, the audience will read the printed materials and ignore you. Handouts that are outlines, visuals only, or slides with just a few bullet points on each can be distributed to the audience in advance, so attendees can write notes directly on them.

Why do you need handouts? They enhance learning. But the main reason to give handouts is to ensure that every attendee (at least some of whom are potential customers, or you wouldn't be addressing the group) walks away with a piece of paper containing information on what you offer and how to contact you.

That way, when the person goes to work the next morning and thinks, "That was an interesting talk; maybe I should contact that speaker to talk about how his firm can help us," he or she has your phone number in hand.

Without a handout, response to your talk will be diminished; most people are too busy, lazy, or indifferent to start tracking you down if they don't have immediate access to your contact information.

Another reason to provide a handout is to further ensure attendee satisfaction. Even with a great seminar, attendees feel they get more value when they walk away with some hard copy reference materials they can share with their team when they get back to work.

It's important to give a useful, interesting, information-packed talk that convinces prospects you know what you are talking about and makes them want to speak with you about doing work for them.

But without the contact information immediately in hand, the prospect's interest and curiosity quickly evaporate. Because you cannot tell in advance who in the audience will want to follow up with you, your goal is to get everybody or as many people as possible to pick up and take home your handout material.

There are several ways to distribute handouts at your talk. The most common is to leave the materials on a table, either in the back of the room or at the registration table where people sign in for the meeting or your session.

But this is not effective. Most people will walk right by the table without picking up the material. Many won't even notice the table or stack of handouts.

Even if you point out the table and say that reprints are available, many won't take one. And you might feel embarrassed at the silence that follows your announcement; it makes you seem less authoritative, more of a promoter.

Another technique is to put a copy of your handout on each seat in the room about a half hour before the start of your presentation. Most people will pick it up, look at it; about one-quarter to one-half will take it with them when they leave, and half or more will leave it on the chair.

Disadvantages? People may read the handout and not pay attention to your presentation. Also, some people resent this approach, seeing it as being too pushy and too salesy, especially if your handout material includes an order form for your products or a brochure about your company and your services.

CHAPTER 64

Elmore Leonard on Becoming a Novelist

My friend Hunter Shea is a successful and prolific horror writer.

He is the author of more than 17 published novels including "The Jersey Devil" (Pinnacle), "They Rise" (Severed Press), and "We Are Always Watching" (Sinister Grin).

Anyway, Hunter recently told me an interesting story with a lesson for writers that I want to share with you now.

Take it away, Mr. Shea....

"I attended only one writer's conference in my life. It was close to home in New York City, held in a college during the semester break.

"Following my printed schedule, I went to a classroom to listen to a famous thriller author talk about his path to publication.

"It was a packed room, so I had to take a seat in the back. I noticed an old man sitting next to me.

"He leaned over and whispered, 'You spend a lot of money on this, kid?'

"'You could say that.' I'd spent nine hundred dollars I didn't have at the time.

"'You see all these people?' he said, pointing at the back of everyone's heads.

"'Yeah.'

"'None of them will ever be writers. Come back here in ten years and you'll see the same faces.

"'Do me a favor. Hold onto your money. You want to be a writer?'

"I nodded, hoping the guy would quiet down once the author started talking.

"'Then go home and do two things. Read a ton. Then write a ton. That's all there is to it.'

"I quietly thanked him for the advice, enjoyed the talk by the thriller author, and attended as many sessions that morning as I could.

"Imagine my surprise when I saw that old man during the lunch event stride up to the podium when he was introduced as the key speaker for the day.

"That man was Elmore Leonard.

"Boom! I took his advice, and never again spent a dime on a writing conference.

"Elmore Leonard saved me enough money over the years to buy a brand new car. I wish he were alive so I could thank him properly.

"If you're going to spend your money, spend it on books to read."

Thanks, Hunter!

CHAPTER 65

Mail Order Days Gone By

A lot of digital marketing today is direct response only done with electrons instead of paper.

As a result of the rise of digital marketing, therefore, direct response has become mainstream.

But back when I got into direct response in the early 80s, it was considered the ugly stepchild of more respectable mainstream Madison advertising.

One reason was that we direct people had the unmitigated gall to want advertising to be profitable and actually sell something with our copy.

Another reason: while Madison Avenue worshipped beautiful graphic design, direct marketers consistently found that "ugly" direct mail worked better than slick and colorful.

The third reason direct marketing was looked down on is that some of the old-time practitioners had a ... well, a penchant for promotion questionable offers.

Promotions that bordered on sleazy. Offers that bordered on being deceptive. Products that were rip-offs.

One of the most famous was the mail order ad that offered "a copper-engraved portrait of America's 16th president" for only $10.

But when you sent in your ten-spot, the marketer fulfilled the order by mailing you a penny.

Another mail order ad of this ilk had the headline, "Gets Rid of Potato Bugs and Other Garden Insects Guaranteed." The product cost $5 in 1969.

When you ordered, you received two blocks of wood with handwritten instructions on how to place the potato bug or other insect on one of the pieces of wood – and squash it with the other.

Says BC, a friend and fellow mail order old-timer: "I laughed so hard, I was in tears."

BC tells this classic mail order story: "A neighbor of our bought a set of lawn furniture for $12. Included 4 chairs, a table and umbrella."

She received the actual scaled size furniture that was in the print ad photo – good for a doll house or a little girl's toy, but not so good for a patio.

BC also reminded me of the mail order ad that sold a vibrating lure designed to help you catch fish like crazy.

BC bought it when he was a kid and says: "I never caught a fish on it. And I guess they have a contest every year and none of the participants have ever caught a fish with it!"

Then there was the ad that said "Turns your closet into a coat room with sturdy metal coat hooks." When you ordered, the marketer sent you a dozen or so nails.

Another classic was "Portable Garage." A plastic tarp you placed over your car to keep the snow and rain off.

The classic of all time is the pet sea monkeys – a vial of brine shrimp eggs that hatched when placed in warm salty water.

As a kid, I actually a lot of fun with the sea monkeys. And I didn't feel ripped off at all!

In fact, the brine shrimp are great live food for tropical fish, which I have kept most of my life.

Although on South Park, Cartman wasn't quite as thrilled as I was with his sea monkeys:

https://www.youtube.com/watch?v=KDNkmsqgIFA

By the way, there is actually a useful, ethical, and legitimate copywriting technique used in the headline "Gets Rid of Potato Bugs and Other Garden Insects Guaranteed."

The headline says "Gets" – and not "Get," as most people would write it.

Why? Because "gets" pulls better.

Reason: "Get rid of" does not omit the possibility that the home owner has to do some or all of the work to eliminate the vermin.

But "gets" implies that the product, not the consumer, does all the work.

And people are lazy, and will buy things that help them avoid doing it.

CHAPTER 66

Seven Ways to Double Your Writing Output

As a practitioner of a Protestant work ethic and semi-workaholic writer, I have long had a fascination for prolific authors.

Isaac Asimov, my writing role model, wrote and talked about his prolificacy frequently, and wrote more than 500 books.

Asimov worked 7 days a week. He though the US Postal Service were slackers because they would not deliver mail on Sunday.

When Barbara Walters asked Asimov what he would do if he found out he had only 6 months to live, he replied without missing a beat: "I'd type faster." My kind of guy!

But not many people know that Asimov's friend and fellow SF author, Robert Silverberg – who never talked about his output – was even more prolific.

According to my research, Silverberg has written under his own name and pseudonyms 966 books.

RL Stine is also impressive at 422 books – and for a time was writing a new Goosebumps every 2 weeks.

Barbara Cartland wrote over 700 romance novels, with total sales of more than a billion copies.

The Guinness Book of World Records says the most published works (books, articles, stories) by one author is 1,084.

That honor belongs to L. Ron Hubbard. His first work was published in February 1934 and the last in March 2006.

Guinness says when it comes to word count, however, English writer Charles Hamilton gets the nod.

He published 100 million words in his lifetime ... the equivalent of 1,200 average-length novels ... though the stories were published mainly in magazines, and not as books.

For many writers, writing faster and increasing their output of saleable material is one of the few ways they can make more money.

All else being equal, if you write twice as fast, you produce twice as much.

And if you sell twice as much writing, you double your writing income, right?

That means if you are making $50,000 as a freelance writer now, boosting your productivity and doubling your output can take you to $100,000 a year.

And I'm sure you could use an extra 50K in annual income, right? I know I could!

So here are a few tips to help you increase your writing productivity and production:

1–Make being prolific a goal in and of itself. Prolific writers want to be prolific and take pride in doing so.

2–You must practice and get good so when you double your speed and output, you do not sacrifice quality. Not one iota.

3–Work longer hours. The great Claude Hopkins, who was the highest-paid copywriter of his era, said he made more money than other copywriters because he worked more hours.

4–Love your work. The most prolific writers are so productive because they absolutely love writing. Even the physical process of keyboarding and watching the words appear on the screen, as I am doing right now.

5–Always have multiple writing projects in the hopper. That way, when you start to run out of steam on project A you simply put it aside and pick up on project B. So you never feel blocked or burned out.

6–Use the right keyboard and writing instrument. As a high-speed touch typist, I am only productive on a desktop PC with a typewriter-style keyboard with raised keys. I am slow as molasses on a laptop with flat keys.

7–Devote your life to writing. The two activities I spend the most time on in my waking hours are writing and reading. Those are the only things I love to do. Yes, there are many things I like to do. But love to do? That's it.

Having just now handed in my 94th book to my publisher, I am a slacker and a piker compared to the authors I have listed above.

But to be fair, writing books was their full-time job. Mine are writing copy for my clients and running a small Internet marketing business. Writing books is my avocation.

And given that it is a sideline, on which I spend only an hour or two a day if that, I am okay with not being in their league.

CHAPTER 67

Are Mobile, Social, and Apps Crap?

Lots of people pontificate about marketing. Always have.

The only problem: they don't know what the heck they are talking about.

My first case in point: a young millennial marketer chastised me for my old-fashioned Website.

Even though it has in fact been optimized for mobile, it was originally designed for desktop.

And my young friend told me, as so many has: "Every consumer uses their mobile to shop online today ... no one uses a desktop."

Makes sense. The only problem: the facts say otherwise.

According to a recently released report from Akimo, almost half of consumers – not all by any stretch – brose with their phone.

But only 1 in 5 – a mere 20% – completes purchase transactions on a mobile!

So I said to my young friend who told me desktop is dead: "Wrongo, Mobile Breath!"

(Being so young, I am sure he didn't get the Johnny Carson connection.)

Second case in point: the much ado about social media nothing.

A study by Riple found that 55% of small business owners listed Facebook posts as their most important marketing tool.

They are apparently unaware of the MediaPost research showing that e-mail is 6 times more likely to generate a direct response than a social post.

Third case in point: The other day, a friend asked me if I had a certain app.

I told him that I have NO apps.

"How can someone in today's mobile age not use apps?" he asked.

My question: If apps are so useful, important, and vital – why does Localytics reports that one in four mobile apps are abandoned after being used just one time?

The lesson for marketers: don't listen to all the hooey and BS out there.

Use what works. Test it for yourself.

Then do more of what works – and less of what doesn't.

Not exactly rocket science, is it?

CHAPTER 68

Secrets of Successful B2B Lead Generation Online

The problem with online B2B lead generation today is that many marketers who do it are not in fact generating sales leads – they are just generating inquiries and giving away free white papers and other content to everyone who asks for it.

What's the difference? It's this: An inquiry is a request for free information from virtually anyone on the planet. A sales lead, by comparison, is an inquiry from a qualified *prospect* – someone who has the *money, authority, and desire* to buy your product.

Anyone can generate an inquiry or response by giving away free stuff, because (a) people love free stuff and (b) they make no commitment and minimal effort to grab it online. It's so easy.

Generating sales leads – inquiries from legitimate prospects – and converting them into orders and customers takes a bit more strategy, planning, and skill. So how do we do it online?

To begin with, there is the matter of what "qualifying questions" to include on the landing page. These are fields on the online form the prospect fills in when he is requesting your free content, which could be anything from a white paper or a special report, to an e-class or Webinar. You can indicate which fields are mandatory and which are optional. A visitor who does not complete a mandatory field is denied access to the download until he provides the missing information.

The argument against putting too many mandatory fields on an online form is the often-quoted rule of thumb that says for each additional field you make the prospect fill in, your conversion rate drops by 10 percent.

The argument in favor of putting more mandatory fields is that it is the only way to separate "suspects" – freebie seekers who just want a white paper – with prospects who may have a real interest in buying your product.

Here are the fields I use on my landing page that give me a better indication of whether a respondent is just a freebie seeker or a real prospect:

- Name – I require the prospect's name. Mandatory.
- Title – prospects with the right title are better qualified. Optional.
- Company name – someone without a real company is for me not a prospect; it may be different for you. Mandatory.
- Phone number – I do not honor inquiries without a phone number, since telephone follow-up is critical to assessing my prospect's needs and determining whether it's a good fit for me. Mandatory.
- E-mail – also a must for e-mail follow up and to add them to my opt-in subscriber list. Mandatory.

- Address, city, state, zip – I don't need this because I don't qualify prospects by geographic location, I work remotely and do not travel to see clients, and I send my sales materials electronically as a PDF. Optional.
- Website URL – so I can see what business the prospect is in and send samples of my work relevant to their industry or product line. Mandatory.

Some Internet users try to get around this by entering fake or incomplete information such "XXXX" in the name field or "1234567" in the phone field. I ignore all such inquiries and do not honor the request for the free content.

The second way I qualify inquiries is by offering three different check box options where the prospect can check one, two, or three, but not none, since this is also mandatory. These are:

- Send me your free lead magnet.
- Send me information on your services.
- Call me to give me an estimate on a potential project or need we have.

If a prospect checks only the first item, we send the lead magnet with the realization that they are not a "hot" prospect. I may rate them higher if all of the other fields, especially company and title, are a good fit for me.

If they check the second box as well as or instead of the first box, they are someone more qualified, as they are asking not for just a freebie but for information on the services I provide. Some do that out of curiosity, and some have an upcoming project for which they are looking for a vendor.

The most qualified prospects check the third box. They have an immediate need and want to initiate a preliminary discussion about it. If we are a good match and they are interested, I prepare and send an estimate, which is our short proposal for doing the work.

Some marketers add additional qualifying questions. For instance, a company selling to hospitals asks how many beds the hospital has, which determines how lucrative the account might potentially be. I understand why they ask, but I would rather capture the key lead information, because when you call or e-mail to follow up, you can ask about number of beds and other qualifying questions then.

My goal is to be able to quickly determine whether this is a sales leads with potential to retain my services while maximizing conversion rates. So I ask as few questions as I can to make that determination, and only make the absolutely critical ones mandatory.

However, if a person fills out the mandatory fields honestly but requests the lead magnet only, I send it. The exception is when the person is clearly a competitor, in which case I have no desire to give away wither my content or my promotional package on my services.

CHAPTER 69

Generational Marketing

Today the marketing trade press is obsessed with marketing to specific generations.

The most ignored generation is probably traditionalists, also known as matures: those born between 1922 and 1945. That's probably because even the youngest matures are over 70, and many of the older ones are either dying out or on a limited fixed income. Exceptions? Of course.

Baby boomers – those of us born between 1946 and 1964 – have faded a bit from the limelight, though in certain fields – financial planning, investment advisors, money managers, reverse mortgages, dietary supplements, health insurance, and health care – they are still a prime target.

Generation X, born between 1965 and 1980, tends to get short shrift because, of all the generations younger than matures, they are the smallest.

The attention goes to generation Y, more commonly referred to as millennials. There are more than twice as many millennials, born 1981 to 2000, as there are gen Xer's.

The youngest group is generation Z, born after 2000. Since they are all toddlers, tweens, or teens as of today, many of their purchase decisions are dictated in some form by their parents, either a "yes" or "no," or by controlling their cash flow through allowance. Yes, many have after-school and summer jobs and therefore some limited discretionary income.

Consumer marketing has long targeted buyers based on age and generation. But B2B is different – or more accurately, it was different. But that's changing rapidly.

When I entered the corporate world working in B2B marketing for a Fortune 500 company in the late 1970s, we did not target our marketing by buyer age or generation.

Instead, we targeted it by a number of different factors. These included:

- Industry (using Standard Industrial Codes).
- Size of company (number of employees, gross revenues).
- Job title, function, and education of prospects.

For instance, in my second job out of college, also for a giant corporation, we sold process equipment to chemical plants. The company targeted senior executives, plant managers, process engineers, and purchasing agents, without knowing or caring how old they were.

There were two reasons why, back in the day, B2B marketers targeted prospects by the bulleted items listed above and not generation.

First, all the media was targeted by B2B demographics and firmographics, especially the trade magazines and mailing lists, which were our two primary marketing channels.

For instance, we often rented the subscriber list of Chemical Engineering magazine, a controlled circulation trade journal which you could subscribe to for free by completing a qualification card or "qual card."

The list was segmented based on how subscribers answered question on the qual card. For instance, if you sold pumps, you could select the names of subscribers who checked off on the qual card that they recommended, specified, or purchased pumps.

But none of the trade magazines in which we advertised asked your age on the qual card. Therefore age or generation was not a selection available on the mailing list data card. Job title? Yes. Generation? No.

The second reason why generational marketing played no role in B2B is that we simply never thought that way. What mattered was who you were in the company, what you did, and what you bought. Not how old you were.

Today, however, the B2B marketing press is obsessed with the buying habits of one generation in particular: millennials. Why?

Again, two reasons. The first is that millennials are the largest group of B2B customers: In 2014, Google reported that 46% of potential buyers researching B2B products were millennials, up from 27% in 2012.[3] Today 73% of millennials are involved in B2B purchase decisions for

---

[3] http://www.inc.com/ryan-jenkins/8-keys-to-selling-to-the-millennial-b2b-buyer.html

their companies, and 34% are the sole decision maker for these purchases.

Second, with so much marketing migrating from offline to online channels, marketers perceive, rightly or wrongly, that millennials are more receptive to digital marketing than older buyers.

There is plenty of evidence, however, to the contrary. For instance, an article in the Washington Post reports that according to a 2014 survey, 87% of college textbooks purchased were print editions vs. only 9% for e-books and 4% for reading online at shared sites.[4]

We have been talking about the "generation gap" since I was a wee lad (I will soon turn 60), and the proliferation of both technology and marketing channels has, if anything, widened this chasm. Example: Despite my nearly four decades of experience in B2B marketing, I doubt I would get hired for any corporate marketing job today – again, for two reasons.

First, in both marketing and IT, there is rampant age discrimination. I have many friends in both fields who, though eminently qualified, were downsized in their late 50s and, now in their early 60s, remain unable to find a new position.

Second, there are so many new marketing channels, and I didn't grow up with most of them. So I am never going

---

[4] https://www.washingtonpost.com/local/why-digital-natives-prefer-reading-in-print-yes-you-read-that-right/2015/02/22/8596ca86-b871-11e4-9423-f3d0a1ec335c_story.html?utm_term=.9a003d68a0bd

to be as comfortable with or conversant in social media marketing as most 20-year-olds. And as far as everything going mobile today, I am old school: I still talk primarily on a landline and work on a desktop Dell PC.

So, how do we B2B marketers sell to the huge group of millennials in charge of B2B buying decisions? In her book *Generation Gaps* (Parkside Publishing), Deanne DeMarco notes, for what it is worth, that millennials:

- Believe relationships are more important than organization.
- Want to have a say in how work gets done.
- Desire open, authentic, constant, and real-time information – which as I see it accounts for the boom in content marketing today.

One more point: a lot of millennials I know scoff at e-mail, preferring to text. But millennials in marketing should keep this in mind: a 2016 survey by the Direct Marketing Association showed that e-mail has a median ROI of 122%, which is 4 times higher than both paid search and social media!

CHAPTER 70

Living in the Idiot's Paradise

This happens to me with some regularity:

A person e-mails to criticize something I have produced – often a book, ebook, info product, or one of my landing pages or Websites.

Sometimes they are nice ... but more often, a bit snarky.

And wouldn't you know it, almost all of these e-mails send the same way: "Hire ME to fix it for you!"

This doesn't work, for 3 reasons.

First, you don't start off any business relationship by insulting the potential client or customer.

Second, the person has only complained. But they have not presented a single shred of evidence that

Third, they think you are unaware of the problem, and that they are somehow doing you a service by bringing it to your attention.

What they do not realize is: we already know about the problem.

We just haven't done anything about it either because (a) we haven't had time, and it is a relatively low priority or (b) we don't agree with them that it is in fact a problem.

And not because we are stupid, lazy, unskilled, or unaware.

For instance, former subscriber (I unsubscribed her) PZ wrote:

"Last week I purchased Writing Brochures for Fun and Profit ebook. Please issue a credit to my PayPal account.

"I'm more than disappointed, this just feels like a rip-off.

"While some of the ideas are still good, referencing mainframes, VCRs, and tape reels is not only ridiculous it's going to send younger readers to Google.

"Below is a copy of my receipt, and screenshots of a couple of the most absurd pages.

And of course, PZ moves in for the close:

"If you are interested in having this and other materials updated, please do get in touch. I do a lot of editing and updating to repurpose old material."

I immediately wrote back:

"Why would I want to hire you? I can't think of a single reason.

"We are going to refund your money, unsubscribe you, block you from our shopping cart and our e-mail inbox.

"PZ, you are starving to death with a loaf of bread under each arm.

"Because what's important is what you said in your e-mail: the ideas are still good.

"Do you reject books like Ogilvy on Advertising, Scientific Advertising, How to Win Friends and Influence People, and the Bible because they were written a few years ago?

"If so, how sad for you. For you are the one missing out. That I didn't update mainframe to distributed computing or whatever has absolutely nothing to do with the value of the course you bought.

"You are foolishly starving to death with a loaf of bread under each arm."

Two important takeaways if you are a buyer of business and marketing advice, a seller of services, or both:

1–Technology is transient. But human psychology has not changed in 10 centuries.

2–Criticizing someone's business and then offering to come in and help them make it better is absolutely the worst prospecting strategy on the planet.

To me, the best I can say about PZ is that she, to turn a phrase from Coolio, is living in the "Idiot's Paradise."

KM, another writer/ignoramus trolling for business, wrote a letter to my friend, RA.

He said RA's direct mail package was terrible, and for a fee, he would rewrite it and make the copy much better.

RA and I had a good laugh over this, because (a) the package was selling the product like hot cakes and (b) it was written by one of the top copywriters in the country – RA himself.

And that's my third takeaway:

3–Talking about stuff without knowing the facts is a good opportunity to make yourself look like a total fool and become yet another resident of Idiot's Paradise.

CHAPTER 71

Little-Known Content Marketing Secret

MS recently downloaded a copy of my Special Report, "Writing Industrial Copy That Sells."

I offer it free to folks interesting in my copywriting services, books, and courses – and MS took advantage of it.

After MS downloaded the free report, he sent this quick e-mail to me in response:

"Hi. Thanks. This is an awesome report – much better than some I've paid for."

And therein lies a simple but powerful marketing lesson:

The content you give away for free should be as good as, or preferably better than, the content you sell!

This may seem counterintuitive.

You think, "Well, the person is not paying. So it doesn't have to be that good. For free, so-so should be good enough."

But the purpose of giving away a free report is to either (a) strengthen your reputation as a subject matter expert or (b) upsell prospects to your paid products or services.

So riddle me this: If I get a report from you, and it's a yawn, then why would I bother to give you money for more of the same level of thinking, expertise, or advice?

And don't tell me, "Well, people know the free stuff is just a taste, but for the steak dinner, they gotta pay the full price."

Because actually, they don't see it that way: If the free sample sucks, you'll almost surely fail to whet their appetite for doing business with you on a paid basis.

That's why the content you give away for free should be as good as, or preferably better than, the content you sell!

But ... just because the free has to be as good or better than the paid, it doesn't have to be the SAME as the paid.

Here's a useful rule of thumb from my colleague WM: The free content tells people WHAT to do.

The paid content or service either tells the how to do it or actually does it for them.

See the difference?

One more time:

Free content is "what to do" ... paid content is "how to do it" ... paid services are "done for you" – doing it for them.

CHAPTER 72

Being Snarky Does Not Pay

Here's a quick and easy communication tip:

Being snarky, rude, sarcastic, or caustic doesn't pay off.

It doesn't help win the other person over to your site.

In fact, it turns them off.

As an example, here's a somewhat snarky e-mail I recently got from subscriber MF.

(It happened to be in response to an essay I wrote about why I prefer writing books for mainstream publishing houses rather than self-publishing.)

He begins:

"Dear Bob: I never buy any of your products."

Already a tad snarky.

"But I do enjoy your e-mails."

That's nicer.

Next, he writes:

"Here are 2 things you seem to be missing about the whole getting a book published process."

Now, MF has every right to disagree with what I say or think – just as I have an equal right to disagree with him.

But whether mainstream is better or worse than self-publishing is, in my opinion, a matter of opinion. Not an indisputable fact one way or the other.

So saying "I disagree with you" is fine. Polite.

But saying "you seem to be missing" is arrogant, rude, and presumptuous – as it assumes he is right and I am wrong, which is exactly what MF did.

Another obnoxious phrase you should avoid in communication is "You failed to," as in, "You failed to do this or that."

Hey, I didn't FAIL to do it.

I either deliberately chose not to do it, deciding it is not worth doing ... or I didn't do it the way you would.

Or maybe I actually didn't do something I was supposed to do.

In that case, just say "you did not do it."

But don't say "failed," as it connotes insult, criticism, and is snarky.

CHAPTER 73

Three Steps to a Great Online Copywriting Portfolio

I recently wrote an article saying I am against copywriters should work "on spec" – with rare exceptions.

Subscriber DW agreed that spec work is a bad idea for writers.

But when she added, "In my opinion, it's right up there with sending prospects samples of your work, and if they like it, they'll pick you."

I immediately replied: "On that, we do not agree."

The fact is, showing potential copywriting clients samples of my published work ... with my current clients' permission, of course ... is a key factor in me making six figures a year for almost 4 decades.

Here is my online copywriting portfolio posted on my site:

http://www.bly.com/newsite/Pages/portfolio.php

Notice 3 important things about my portfolio:

>> First, it's big. Really big. I don't know of a copywriter who has more samples posted online than I do, although there may be – I haven't looked hard.

By having so many samples, I increase the odds that I have something online that will impress the client and make him want to hire me.

>> Second, it's organized in two sections: one by media (e.g., brochures, landing pages, white papers) and the second by product or industry (e.g., financial, health care, software).

For the client who, unbeknownst to me, is browsing my site, this makes it easier for him to find what he is looking for.

>> Third, each sample has a unique clickable hyperlink that I can cut and paste into an e-mail or document.

This allows me to send to clients I am in contact with the samples that best fit their needs and interests within a minute or two – by pasting their URLs into an e-mail and sending it to the prospect.

I have constructed my online portfolio this way because if a sample is well written and generated good response, the closer the sample is to what the client wants me to write for them, the more likely I am to be hired, all else being equal.

Yes, I understand that, when you are a newbie (I never use the term "copy cub"), you don't have a lot of samples at the beginning of your career.

But my advice is you get samples of all your good stuff ... ask the client's permission to post them on your site ... and build a bigger portfolio rather than a smaller one, as quickly as you can.

Two warnings: Never post or share a sample of your work unless the client has given you the okay.

And never post a promotion that you did not in fact write.

Aside from being completely unethical, for all you know the prospect you are showing it to wrote, copy-chiefed, or produced the purloined promotion!

Also, several of my subscribers asked me, "What are your exceptions of your stand against spec work, Bob."

There are only 2 situations in which I say it is OK to do spec work.

The first is spec assignments for marketers looking for copywriters at the annual AWAI Boot Camp Job Fair.

The second is writing a fundraising letter, build your portfolio, for a local nonprofit whose cause you feel strongly about.

That's about it.

CHAPTER 74

Marketing Terms I Like and Don't Like

I know instantly whether a potential copywriting client and I are simpatico just by the marketing terms he or she uses.

For instance, when I hear a client use words like "response" ... "conversion" ... "click-through rates" ... "break-even" ... "results" ... "leads" ... "sales" ... "selling" ... "offer" ... "closing" ... "call to action" ... or "profits" ...

... I know we pray from the same hymnal of direct response.

It's only when clients use other marketing words that my radar signals we might not be a good fit.

For instance, it was trendy for a time to say that marketing is having "conversations" and not selling.

When I wrote about conversations in this e-newsletter, subscriber WM replied:

"I am a salesman. At the end of the month, my sales manager asks me how much I sold. If I was to reply, 'I didn't sell anything, but I had a lot of conversations' – I'd be out on the street."

I'm not saying conversations are not a valid part of the sales and marketing process.

But marketers who focus on "conversation" sometimes do so to avoid revealing that they do not know how to write copy that sells.

"Branding" always makes me a bit wary. Yes, it's also a valid and often important part of marketing.

But in marketing speak, it's often code for, "We just position our product in the marketplace but don't know how to sell."

And "brand awareness" is sometimes code for, "I talk about awareness because it can't really be measured and therefore I am shielded from having to produce a result that can be measured, which would reveal whether my ad is working and profitable."

For many years, "content" didn't sit well with me, as I thought it devalued and positioned writing as a commodity – just as calling a writer a "word smith" did back in the day.

But content has become an accepted term, and I am good with it now.

Same with "content marketing," which we used to call "getting more leads and sales by giving away free information."

The title "content marketing strategist" though is a bit overblown to me, as many (not all) people who call themselves that essentially just write online articles for clients.

"Impressions" is another term I shy away from. I am not trying to impress anyone. I am trying to sell them a product or service.

"Likes," "followers," and "connections" in social media. Well, they are valid and measurable, and have some value.

But they are nothing to get excited about, if they are not driving traffic, converting, and filling up your PayPal account with money from customer orders.

Any particular marketing terms you like or don't like? And do you agree or disagree with my assessment of marketing lingo here?

For an up-to-date glossary of marketing terms, see my book "Marketing Dictionary for the 21st Century," published by Motivational Press.

CHAPTER 75

The Bright Shiny Object Syndrome

Today many people – and believe in particular, many younger people – are fascinated with bright, shiny objects (BSOs).

By "BSO," I mean they embrace the new, trendy, hip, and cool ... and as a corollary, eschew the old, the proven, and the tried and true.

This favoring of BSOs over tested methods and ideas is true in many fields, but especially so in marketing.

I contend that doing so is an egregious error.

Why?

Two reasons.

First, to paraphrase George Santayana – "Those who forget the past, don't learn from it."

Or more to the point, as Martin Cohen writes in his book Reason and Nature:

"The notion that we can dismiss the views of all previous thinkers surely leaves no basis for the hope that our own work will prove of any value to others."

To me this is "axiomatic," which means it is irrefutable logic and always true.

Think about it: if you dismiss the views of all who came before you, then shouldn't the next generation conclude they can learn nothing from you?

Second, the problem with BSOs is: they are untested and unproven.

That makes them highly risky and more likely to fail.

By comparison, the tried and true is tested and proven.

That reduces your risk of a big failure ... and increases the odds of success.

How does this translate into direct marketing?

Well, many times I have come up with an initial selling idea for a product.

When I run it past the client, they say – "That won't work; we know because we have tested it many times, and in each test it always failed."

A BSO fan would argue:

"Well, just because you guys couldn't get it to work doesn't mean it won't work now. Get some cojones and try it my way."

As a tried and true fan, I am grateful the client knows the idea has been tested and proven ineffective, as it saves me from writing something that will more than likely bomb.

I thank them, go back to the drawing board, and brainstorm, both on my own and often with them, to find a new idea with the potential to be a winner.

Other old-time direct response copywriters tell me they agree that the surest and most likely route to a winner is to take what is tested and proven, dust it off, and give it a new twist.

In copywriting, it is rare to find something under the sun that is entirely new.

More often, winning comes from saying the same old thing, but saying it in a fresh and compelling new way.

And then test, test, test.

Don't assume your idea, whether old school or BSO, is the best.

You don't know. You have to test.

In marketing, as the great Claude Hopkins wrote: The only way to settle the question of whether an ad will work is with a test, not with arguments around a table.

And then, once we direct marketers roll it out, while continually testing to beat our control.

Back in my day, people at Madison Avenue ad agencies hated the tested direct response control.

They believed in their intuition and subjective judgment of their peers: If everyone at the agency or my friends in advertising think my ad is clever, funny, or creative, it must be good!

This in part explains the gross ineffectiveness of so many widely admired national ad campaigns for major brands produced by the big ad agencies.

My friend, motivational Rob Gilbert, says the key to success in virtually every walk of life is:

"Do more of what works, and less of what doesn't work."

Pretty simple. Common sense. And good advice.

CHAPTER 76

Profit from the "Knowledge Business"

There's a lot of money in teaching the business, tasks, and skills you have mastered ... and the information you have researched, learned, and produced ... to others who seek to learn them.

Collectively this is the "knowledge business" – packaging your knowledge as products and services to sell for a price.

Including: ebooks ... newsletters ... special reports ... books ... online courses ... Webinars ... seminars ... college courses ... conferences ... boot camps ... coaching ... consulting ... DVDs ... audio CD albums ... training ... membership sites ... Facebook groups ... the list goes on and on.

So, how it possible that a "knowledge business" even exists? What makes it possible?

The key to it all a simple principle George Clason wrote about in his book The Richest Man in Babylon:

"That which one man knows can be taught to others."

That's the premise – proven since the dawn of humankind – on which today's knowledge business is based.

Now, some who want to get into the knowledge business protest, "But I am just ordinary; I don't know anything others will pay for."

This is almost never the case.

As Dr. Gary North warns: "The great mistake of most small business people is to imagine that their detailed knowledge of their niche market is widely dispersed.

"On the contrary, hardly anyone knows it. They are owners of a capital asset that others do not possess and have no easy way of possessing it."

And will therefore pay handsomely to obtain.

Another objection I hear is: "Well, I know something about topic X. But I am not the world's leading expert. So how can I presume to teach others?"

Info marketing guru Fred Gleeck astutely notes:

"You don't have to know more about your topic than anyone else in the world. You just have to know more than 90% of the people in the world."

And either you do now or can get to that level with some work.

Widely quotes research shows it only takes 1,000 hours to be competent at something and 10,000 hours to become a master of it.

Also, if you both know the subject and how to teach it to others, you are a better source of knowledge transfer than other experts who perhaps knows more than you – but are lousy teachers, as so many are.

The next objection is: "There is so much information available for free on my topic already on the Internet, why would anyone pay me for the same information they can already get the same stuff on the Web at no cost?"

Here's the thing: What is widely available online is just data and information.

But in the knowledge business, we don't merely sell data and information ... although, both are usually part of our offerings.

What sets us apart is our paid info products and services provide:

>> Data we have collected through long effort that others in fact do not have.

>> Deep knowledge gleaned from our data and long experience.

>> Analysis of the data and knowledge to show what it means and how our customers can benefit from it.

>> Actionable ideas tested and proven to enable those using them to achieve the desired results.

>> Wisdom to understand what will work in a field, what won't, and to consistently know the difference.

In other words, mere data and information are often free for the asking.

But actionable ideas on how people can use it for their gain is in short supply ... and again, people will pay you handsomely to get this knowledge.

One more fact about the knowledge business:

If you gain a wide fan base and become a recognized authority in your field, people will pay a premium for your knowledge. If you don't, they are less likely to do so.

To master a proven methodology for becoming an instant guru, read my book *Become a Recognized Authority in Your Field in 60 Days or Less*, published by Alpha Books.

CHAPTER 77

Three Little Lists That Can Double Your Productivity

There are a lot of gadgets, devices, apps, and software packages today people use to keep organized, manage their time, and boost their personal productivity.

But I don't use them.

Instead, I'm going to give you my top personal productivity methodology right now for free.

I use the system with Word – but in a pinch, a pencil and paper will do just fine.

This is sort of a "personal productivity by the numbers" approach based on having just 3 simple to-do lists and updating them weekly; keeping them as Word files on my hard drive makes the updating – and printing of the revised lists – quick and easy.

You can use more or fewer lists. You can use different lists than mine. But the multi-list principle is the same.

Here are my lists:

#1: To-Do Today List ... This is a list of all current copywriting projects I am working one for my clients.

It is arranged so that the project with the closest deadline is number one on the list, the project with the next-closest deadline is number two, and so on.

This list I actually update several times a week, and sometimes daily, based on my progress and completion on the various copywriting assignments.

I begin with day by immediately working on item #1 on the list.

When I am unable to continue because either I am tiring or there is an obstacle preventing me from doing so (e.g., I am waiting for a client to provide a promised and important background document, comments on a draft, etc.), I move on to the next item in the list.

By having multiple projects and handling them in this fashion, I maximize my productivity:

When I run out of steam on number one from the list, I put it aside and move to number two.

So I am always fresh and energized; never bored. And can therefore write better and faster.

I break my day into one-hour writing increments, taking a 3 to 5 minute break at the end of each hour to refill coffee or watch Elvis or Dire Straits on a YouTube Clip.

Then I decide after completion of an hour module and during this break whether to continue with that project or switch gears and work on another.

#2: To-Do Bob Projects: This is a list of all the projects I have in some stage of development from "it seems a good idea" to "currently in progress."

These projects include: books ... information products ... columns ... articles ... seminars, speeches, workshops, and conferences ... and other projects.

#3: To-Come List ... This is a list of my sales leads: marketers who have reached out to me and expressed interest in hiring me to write copy.

I annotate the to-come list to note which leads are the best fit for me, which have an immediate need, and which just want to know more about me for possible future work.

These prospects are simply listed in descending order of date of first contact, with the most recent leads at top.

The To-Do Today List is my priority, because contract freelance copywriting is my main source of income, my bread and butter, and clients come first.

My second priority is my own projects. I usually work on these during the final hour or so of my 12-hour day, as a way of chilling and winding down.

Third comes tracking sales leads and talking with potential clients, because my first obligation is to my current clients and projects; I can't detract from that focus by diverting attention and energy to potential new business.

And that's my 3-list personal productivity system in a nutshell: simple, easy and it works.

CHAPTER 78

To Get More Done, Grab Some Zzzs

In Chapter 77, I give you my #1 personal productivity tip: making simple to-do lists.

My #2 personal productivity tip is also deceptively simple: get enough sleep.

Forget the average; you know how much sleep you need to get enough rest for peak performance the next day.

For me, it is about 8 hours or a tad more. Nine is too much, seven is adequate in a pinch, and with six or fewer I'm dragging the next day.

Now here's the secret of this tip: actually get the hours of sleep you need – every night the next day is a full work day.

Sounds easy, but most people don't do it.

Here's how I ensure adequate sleep for maximum productivity, and some of these ideas my work for you too:

1–I believe in early to bed, early to rise.

Why?

When you get up early, by the time 9am rolls around, you've already done a pile of work. So the pressure is off.

On the other hand, if you delay doing the work until night, you may get distracted and never get to it at all.

Because I need 8 hours, I go to bed around 10pm, and rise and start working at 6am.

2–Don't go out weeknights.

With rare exception, I do not go out weeknights – no meetings, no bowling, no poker game, no activities outside the home of any kind.

When you go out, it is likely you will not go to bed until late, which will adversely affect energy and productivity for the next day.

3–Don't eat too late.

A big meal too close to bedtime can cause you to sleep poorly and not feel well.

(Overeating in general makes you lethargic.)

4–Always make sure you get your full sleep.

On the rare occasion when circumstance forces me to go to bed later than my normal time, I also – unless my schedule absolutely makes it impossible – get up later.

I hate starting late. But working without enough sleep would cut into my productive hours, so the net output would be even worse.

5–Don't forget to prepare tomorrow's list of things to do tonight.

At the end of the day, I prepare my to-do lists for the next day and post it on my bulletin board before shutting down for the night.

If you don't, you risk thinking, worrying, and ruminating about work and all you have to do.

I also place the file for the first task I will do tomorrow on a stand next to my desk.

This way, I can start working the instant I step into the office the next morning – and I like a quick start.

CHAPTER 79

Subjective Judgment in Reviewing Copy

One of the most nonsensical – and fairly common – conversations in marketing goes something like this....

The ad agency or copywriter submits a promotion.

The client says, "I don't like it."

The copywriter gets his dander up, bristles, and says belligerently:

"It's very strong. Test it."

The client refuses.

The copywriter goes on Facebook and says:

"I have a stupid client who refuses to A/B split test."

Other copywriters chime in and say the client is stupid.

But ... in fact, he is not stupid.

Most of the time, the client is well aware that the A/B split test is the only legitimate way to test a promotion.

The reason this is so is because only a marketing test definitively determines whether the copy is strong based on results, and not on subjective judgment.

But despite this fact, subjective judgment will always be part of the process of developing marketing campaigns. Reason:

Before your copy can be tested in an A/B split, the team has to agree on pricing ... offer ... theme ... bonuses ...

lists ... the "big idea" for the promotion ... the headline ... the lead ... and more.

"Pre-test" and screening of what to ultimately prepare and test for real with money has to come down to subjective judgment.

Now, you've heard the old express, "Opinions are like A-holes; everybody has one."

But of those opinions, the one that counts the most is the client's, not yours, because he is paying the bills and putting his money on the line.

And having the final say does not make him an A-hole. Far from it.

Fact of the matter is, you may in fact know more about copywriting than your client (although in some cases, not).

But the client almost certainly knows more about his business than you.

Therefore, his instincts and opinions should be considered carefully, and never ignored or dismissed by you out of hand.

Now, if you feel strongly that nothing beats your copy, and client criticism annoys you, start your own online information marketing business.

When it's your business, you can run all your copy exactly as you wrote it.

But if having the final say is paramount, you should only be an entrepreneur who writes his own copy.

And not a freelancer writing for clients.

A number of copywriters have made the transition from doing client work to 100% writing copy for their own products.

Nothing wrong with that. More power to them. I know several, and a few are almost militant about why theirs is the smarter copywriting path.

As an ancillary income stream, I also write copy to sell info products I publish online.

And it by itself generates a six-figure annual income we could comfortably live on.

But that's not the way I roll.

Writing copy for clients has pleasures and intellectual challenges I maintain you simply cannot get from writing only about your own products.

And as a contract copywriting freelance, I absolutely love the wide variety of products, services, offers, industrial, and markets I get to write about and for.

It's more fun than I can shake a stick at.

So overall, no complaints – though on rare occasion I may grumble a bit.

But for nearly 4 decades, I have been primarily a traditional copywriter working for clients.

And secondarily an info marketer, book author, consultant, and speaker.

And that's where I want to be in my copywriting business:

As I have done what I wanted to, likewise, you should do what works for you.

As the late, great David Ogilvy said, quoting an old Scottish proverb:

"Be happy while you're living, for you're a long time dead."

CHAPTER 80

On Being Nice

I used to think, until recently, it always paid off to be nice to everyone, or at least was the right thing to do.

But something happened recently that made me think that maybe this should not apply to everyone in your life.

Here's the story ... and the one category of people I might no longer apply my "always be nice" rule to:

When our new and expensive central air conditioner seemed to be underperforming, I called CC, the HVAC contractor that installed it.

I took a premium AC unit, deluxe model, new custom duct work, full warranty, and covered by 24/7 service.

And I paid a premium price for it.

So when the AC seemed to be underperforming on a hot summer night, I called CC.

Mike, their on-call emergency tech responded, said he was at another job, and as soon as he was done with that customer, he would call me, which he did.

At that point, it was night, the house was more comfortable, and so I figured I could give Mike a break.

I told Mike to knock off early and go home – provided another CC tech could come first thing in the morning, before the house heated up again.

He said OK. But when I called CC the next morning, I was told, "The day service shift is on a big commercial job now, so they cannot come until afternoon."

Not a big deal, I know. So I did not make a fuss.

But look: If I had been a bad guy, and insisted Mike come and work late, my AC would have been fixed on the spot. I would have gotten what I wanted.

Now, with another hot day, I was going to pay for my courtesy and kindness by being made to swelter and wait.

Hardly seems fair to me, right?

As a rule, it does us, as businesspeople as well as consumers, to be nice rather than nasty or even difficult.

That includes being nice to everyone you deal with professionally – clients, employees, and vendors like CC.

Well, I feel I have to be nice to clients, and I usually am.

But the day after the CC incident, I was considering that maybe with vendors and others who sell services to me, being nice all the time is a little less critical.

I was ultra-nice to Mike at CC. And in return, I was penalized for it.

So what's a nice guy to do?

I think I'll keep being nice, because life is too short to be an a-hole.

Although I sometimes am, despite my best efforts to the contrary.

One more point....

If you are a service provider like CC, and a customer is nice to you, and cuts you some slack, if anything you should show appreciation – a short e-mail, a note, or maybe a certificate for $20 off the next service or product you buy from them or Starbucks.

Right?

CHAPTER 81

The Fallacy of Being the Highest Price

I recently told BL, a colleague, that I was pretty busy with copywriting assignments (I usually am).

Like so many people, he immediately said, "You should raise your prices!"

"Thanks, but no thanks," I replied.

Like BL, many people say you should raise your prices when you are so busy with orders at your current prices that you can't take on any more business.

The logic is that being so busy gives you leverage to make prices higher, because if some customers balk at the new higher price tags, you can afford to let them walk, being as busy and successful as you are.

However, I don't see being busy as an opportunity to charge more ... for 2 reasons.

First, it's a form of price gouging.

Those who tell me to raise my prices, BL and other top people in my fields of copywriting and info marketing, prefer to always extract as much money from every client as they can.

They firmly believe that too little believe that you should charge the customer as much as you can, as much as they possibly can afford to pay.

I do not agree.

I prefer to charge a fair and reasonable price for the product or service I provide.

But not more than that.

I know I don't like it when a vendor – even one in high demand and therefore arguably in a positon of power – squeezes me for every last dime they can get.

If you don't like when sellers charge you outrageously high fees, rest assured your customers don't like it either.

And I won't do unto my clients what I don't want others to do unto me.

Even if it's perfectly legal to do so, it is at best unkindly and at worst morally reprehensible to take buyers for every last nickel they have.

Like the pharmaceutical executive who overnight raised the price of the life-saving drug, which only his firm could supply, tenfold ... so that many chronically ill people who needed it to live could no longer afford to buy it.

In the lending industry, you can't just charge any interest rates you want. The rate is limited by law.

To make loans above the legal rate limit is called "usury" or charging "usurious" rates.

And usury is actually a crime.

Second, charging prices that are affordable to your customers, is not only appreciated by them – it's also good for your customer retention rate, repeat business, referrals, and reorders.

DM, another colleague, once said to me that if a freelance direct response copywriter (which DM was) charged an outrageously high fee ... and the promotion she wrote was anything other than a grand-slam home run ...

... the client would resent the gouging, and never hire that freelance writer again ... which had in fact happened in the case of the other writer we were discussing, who had just done this with one of DM's clients.

Years ago, GD, a pricing consultant, told me that in a service business, you should charge a price in the middle of the top third of providers.

His logic was as follows:

If your fee is in the bottom third, prospects assume you aren't any good.

After all, if you were any good, you would be charging more, right?

GD also said that if you charged in the middle third, again you would be viewed as midlevel in talent and skills – and prospects want the best service provider, not a mediocre one.

So your price should be in the upper third of the cost spectrum.

But, if it's at the top of the upper third, your price is then so high that you make difficult for clients to give you repeat business.

Because your prices are so high, clients cringe whenever you quote a fee ... and begin looking for another good professional who charges perhaps a bit less to replace you.

However, if your clients like you and your work, and you charge in the middle of the top third, they will pay what you ask – and not run every time you send an estimate to get other quotes.

And if you can get top dollar without losing clients with pricing in the middle of the top third, there is no reason to lower your fees to the bottom of the top third, right?

CHAPTER 82

How to Ethically be the High-Priced Provider

In my last essay, I preached against price gouging.

But there are times when it is not only ethical to charge top dollar ... but when customers will readily and even gladly pay it.

And once of those times is when you add extra value to your offering.

For instance, a few weeks ago, I wrote about CC, the HVAC contractor who put in our new central air conditioning system.

I had gotten estimates from three HVAC companies for the new AC – one from CC, one from AA, and one from BB.

Theirs was the highest, which based on the common misconception some people have that the low-priced bidder always wins, would mean they didn't get the sale.

But in fact, I chose CC, even though both competitors charged one or two grand less for a central AC of the same size and comparable quality (major brand).

Why?

Because CC offered something AA and BB do not: 24/7 on-call emergency service.

Meaning if your central AC system fails, they will come out to fix it at any time of the day or night – even Sundays and holidays.

Why did this value-added service tip my decision in their favor?

Because I am miserable in hot weather without AC and cannot abide to be without it even for brief periods.

All companies – CC, AA, and BB – gave a 10-year warranty.

But only CC is available to perform service, warranty or otherwise, around the clock.

And when the temperature outside is 90 degrees F, I want my AC fixed and working immediately – not tomorrow.

In my town, CC is the only HVAC contractor offering round-the-clock service for central air.

And for me, an extra one or two grand up-front is a drop in the bucket compared with the productivity decrease I'd suffer (I work at home) on a hot day if the AC were to be out for more than a couple of hours.

Having said that, having the high price does not guarantee people will view you as the superior value-added vendor, either.

For instance, having uninterrupted electric power is even more important to me than uninterrupted AC.

So we asked three contractors to give us estimates for a new whole-house back-up generator running on natural gas from the utility company.

Two quotes were very close in price. But the third, from contractor JD, was almost 50% higher – almost 6 grand more.

JD explained that his system designs (the machine is the same as the other contractors) are more intelligent, reliable, and better-performing.

But instead of backing this up with documented proof, customer testimonials, or a plausible explanation of why his was worth its premium price, he spouted technical gibberish that even I, with a BS in engineering, could not understand.

When he could see I wasn't buying, he became highly agitated, and began ranting about how stupid I would be to go with his competitors.

I felt he was sincere and probably legitimate – a guy who knows his trade.

But he had failed to prove his case for deserving a higher fee to me.

And so he lost the sale with me, as I suspect he has many times before.

Bottom line: It's not whether you are the high or low price that determines whether you make the sale.

But if you are not the low bidder, it's whether the premium price you are asking is a drop in the buckets compared to the added value you deliver.

And also whether you can back-up and prove the alleged superiority of your offering.

CHAPTER 83

The One Thing in Marketing
That Never, Ever Changes

"Bob, I am trying to read some of the classic marketing books you recommend, such as those written by David Ogilvy, Claude Hopkins, John Caples, Robert Collier, and Vic Schwab.

"But all the examples in them are print ads, and it's hard for me to see how these relate to app banners or e-mail follow-up sequences."

I hear this a lot from millennial marketers: They believe that the rapid pace of change has made the marketing of the 20th century irrelevant to marketing in the 21st century.

Here's why such thinking is fallacious:

Yes, the technology, media, and methods – newspapers and network TV commercial vs. social media, programmatic advertising, and hyperlocal marketing – are much different today than they were yesterday.

But the core of marketing is not channels, technology, databases, or media.

Rather, the most important element of marketing and selling is human psychology – or more specifically, the psychology of persuasion.

And human psychology has not changed in ten centuries.

That means the core persuasion techniques of Ogilvy, Caples, and the other master marketers whose books I recommend have not lost one microdot of their power and effectiveness.

And here are the 10 books I fervently believe every marketer, and that goes especially for you young folk, should devout:

1–"How to Write a Good Advertisement" by Vic Schwab, Wilshire Book Company. A common-sense course in how to write advertising copy that gets people to buy your product or service, written by a plain-speaking veteran mail order copywriter in 1960.

2–"My First 50 Years in Advertising" by Max Sackheim, Prentice-Hall. Another plain-speaking, common-sense guide that stresses salesmanship over creativity, and results over awards. The author was one of the originators of the Book of the Month Club.

3–"The Robert Collier Letter Book" by Robert Collier, Important Books. While Schwab and Sackheim concentrate on space ads, Collier focuses on the art of writing sales letters. While some of the letters may seem old-fashioned and dated, Collier's timeless principles still apply.

4–"Reality in Advertising" by Rosser Reeves, Alfred A. Knopf. The book in which Reeves introduced the now-famous concept of Unique Selling Proposition or USP.

5–"Breakthrough Advertising" by Eugene Schwartz, Boardroom. A copywriting guide by one of the greatest direct-response copywriters of the 20th century.

6–"Tested Advertising Methods" by John Caples, Prentice-Hall. Presents the principles of persuasion as proven through A/B spit tests.

7–"Confessions of an Advertising Man" by David Ogilvy, Atheneum. Charming autobiography of legendary ad man David Ogilvy, packed with useful advice on how to create effective advertising.

8–"Scientific Advertising" by Claude Hopkins, Bell Publishing. A book on the philosophy that advertising's purpose is to sell, not entertain or win creative awards – and how to apply this philosophy to create winning ads.

9–"Method Marketing" by Denny Hatch, Bonus Books. A book on how to write successful direct response copy by putting yourself in the customer's shoes. Packed with cases.

10–"Advertising Secrets of the Written Word" by Joseph Sugarman, DelStar. How to write ad copy by a master of mail order advertising.

Have I left any out? Yes, many. But this list is a good start.

How many have you read? If not all, you ignore them at your own peril.

CHAPTER 84

Bleak Job Prospects for Content Writers and Journalists

We recently saw War of the Planet of the Apes, where intelligent apes take over as the dominant species of our planet.

Well, it's happening ... only instead of apes taking over, it's smartphones and laptops!

According to an article in ClickZ, Gartner predicts that by 2018, 20% of all business content will be written by machine.

In July 2017, Google invested over $800,000 in the Press Association's initiative to generate news stories solely through the use of AI.

The frightening future for writers is that AI machines may make us totally obsolete by doing our jobs as well or better than we can – and for a lot less money.

In China, human customer service representatives who handle live chatbot calls are now being replaced by algorithms.

[x]cube, a maker of automated chatbots, says that 34% of businesses surveyed believe that half of all customer service calls could be handled by robot chatbots without a human agent.

In his book The Rise of the Robots, Martin Ford reprints a perfectly adequate sports article and then reveals it was written entirely by computer – without the touch of a human hand. It's not spectacular, but it's more than competent.

Swedish programmer Sverker Johansson built an AI writing algorithm that has authored nearly 3 million articles now posted on Wikipedia.

And it's not just writers or customer service reps who are in danger of losing their jobs to a computer.

Elon Musk believes that by 2030 to 2040 computers will be able to do anything a human can do.

It makes me wonder why Musk, Google, the Chinese AI chatbot maker, and other clever tech entrepreneurs are so darn eager to put billions of human beings permanently out of work.

Years ago, I had this debate with AN, an old college friend.

AN gave the party line comment about automation and robotics "freeing" people from dull, repetitive jobs so they can do other more rewarding and creative work.

What AN and others miss is this: there are a number of people who don't have the skills or ability or the drive to do work at a higher level than the "dull, repetitive" jobs they hold now.

So when you "free" them from their current boring jobs, you move them into permanent and boring unemployment.

For instance, in the early 1960s, as a kid my mom would take me to visit my dad at work.

His building in downtown Paterson, NJ had a manual elevator run by Joe, a friendly elevator operator who was also nice to me, because he was kind to kids.

One day mom and I went to visit dad, and Joe was gone.

"Where's Joe?" I asked.

She pointed to the self-service buttons labeled G and 1 – 5 on the control panel of the new shiny automatic elevator that had replaced the creaky old manual – and eliminated Joe's job.

"What's Joe going to do?" I asked.

She shrugged.

So I still think about what happened to Joe. He was older, and I suspect he had trouble finding another job, if he was able to at all.

And I also think about what will happen to us in 2040 if Musk is right.

And he probably will be, even if his date comes a little sooner or a little later.

4 Bonus Reports (a $116 Value) – Yours FREE

The essays in this book were originally published in my e-newsletter The Direct Response Letter.

You can get all my new essays for free without buying a thing by subscribing to my free e-newsletter now: www.bly.com/reports

Subscribe now and you also get 4 free bonus reports totaling over 200 pages of actionable how-to marketing content (total value: $116):

** Free Special Report #1: Make $100,000 a Year Selling Information Online.

** Free Special Report #2: Secrets of Successful Business-to-Business Marketing.

** Free Special Report #3: How to Double Your Response Rates.

** Free Special Report #4: Online Marketing That Works.

Each report has a list price of $29; total value of this package of reports is $116.

But you can get all 4 reports FREE when you click on the link below now: www.bly.com/reports

About the Author

BOB BLY is a freelance copywriter with nearly 4 decades of experience in business-to-business and direct marketing. McGraw-Hill calls Bob Bly "America's top copywriter." Clients include IBM, the Conference Board, PSE&G, AT&T, Ott-Lite Technology, Intuit, ExecuNet, Boardroom, Medical Economics, Grumman, RCA, ITT Fluid Technology, and Praxair.

Bob has given presentations to numerous organizations including: National Speakers Association, American Seminar Leaders Association, American Society for Training and Development, U.S. Army, American Society of Journalists and Authors, Society for Technical Communications, Discover Card, Learning Annex, and New York University School of Continuing Education.

He is the author of more than 90 books including *Selling Your Services* (Henry Holt) and *The Elements of Business Writing* (Pearson). Bob's articles have appeared in *Cosmopolitan, Writer's Digest, Successful Meetings, Amtrak Express, Direct, City Paper, New Jersey Monthly,* and many other publications.

Bob writes a monthly column for *Target Marketing* magazine. *The Direct Response Letter*, Bob's monthly e-newsletter, has 65,000 subscribers.

Awards include a Gold Echo from the Direct Marketing Association, an IMMY from the Information Industry Association, two Southstar Awards, an American

Corporate Identity Award of Excellence, the Standard of Excellence award from the Web Marketing Association, Marketer of the Year from Early to Rise, Honorable Mention at the New York Book Festival, and Copywriter of the Year from AWAI.

Bob is a member of the Specialized Information Publishers Association (SIPA) and the American Institute for Chemical Engineers (AIChE). He can be reached at:

Bob Bly
Copywriter
31 Cheyenne Drive
Montville, NJ 07045
Phone: 973-263-0562
Fax: 973-263-0613
E-mail: rwbly@bly.com
Web: www.bly.com

Made in the USA
Lexington, KY
18 August 2017